THE
DIVINE
HANDSHAKE

MANNY RIVERA

THE DIVINE HANDSHAKE

*Partnering with Heaven to
Fulfill God's Purpose*

FOREWORD BY JIM HENNESY

PALMETTO
PUBLISHING
Charleston, SC
www.PalmettoPublishing.com

Copyright © 2024 by Manny Rivera

All rights reserved

No portion of this book may be reproduced, stored in a retrieval system, or transmitted in any form by any means–electronic, mechanical, photocopy, recording, or other–except for brief quotations in printed reviews, without prior permission of the author.

Paperback ISBN: 9798822964891

Table of Contents

Introduction vii
Foreword xiii
Chapter 1:   The Handshake 1
Chapter 2:   The Blank Checks of Friendship 15
Chapter 3:   The Desires of Our Heart 27
Chapter 4:   Co-laboring Requires Alignment 40
Chapter 5:   The Handshake and the House of God 56
Chapter 6:   The Venue of the Handshake: |
             Where Divine and Human Purpose Align 76
Chapter 7:   The Divine Handshake Breaks the Orphan Mindset . . . 83
Chapter 8:   The Framework of the Divine Handshake 102
Chapter 9:   Heaven's Invitation—Stepping into
             the Divine Handshake 115
Chapter 10: The Bold Partnership—Making Big Plans with God . . . 135
Chapter 11: The Dynamic Partnership of
             Prayer and Divine Purpose 147
Chapter 12: The Legacy of Co-Laboring with God 154
Appendix 159
About the Author 163

Introduction

The Divine Handshake—Co-Laboring with God Under an Open Heaven

In Spring 2024, my wife, Victoria, and I traveled to Rome, Italy, to speak at a conference. During our time there, we did as Romans do: we ate pasta, shopped, and visited the sites. I love the subject of history, especially the history of the church. One of my highlights was the tour of the Vatican City Museum. We took our time and enjoyed each area of the museum. The museum tour ended at the Sistine Chapel. There, I received the inspiration to write, compile, and structure this book.

In the center of the Sistine Chapel ceiling is an iconic fresco that has captivated hearts and minds for centuries: Michelangelo's *The Creation of Adam*. In this powerful image, we see the hand of God the Father extending toward Adam, His newly formed creation. God's hand is stretched out with purpose and intention, His finger reaching forward, just inches away from Adam's hand, which is also outstretched but relaxed and waiting. This artwork is not just a portrayal of the creation story. Still, it is a profound representation of divine invitation—God reaching out to humanity, calling us to engage in a divine partnership. This image is a beautiful metaphor for the divine handshake—a symbol of God extending His hand to us, inviting us to co-labor with Him under an open heaven.

The Significance of God's Outstretched Hand

In *The Creation of Adam*, God's hand is active, intentional, and energetic. It signifies God's desire to connect with humanity, empower us, and establish a relationship beyond mere existence. It is a picture of a Father who is passionate about His creation, longing for intimacy and partnership. This divine gesture symbolizes the relationship God desires with each of us—a relationship characterized by communion, collaboration, and co-laboring.

This book, *The Divine Handshake*, delves into the profound implications of that divine gesture. It explores what it means to co-labor with God and to live under an open heaven where His presence, power, and purposes flow freely. Like Michelangelo's depiction of God and Adam almost touching, we are invited to close the gap, to reach out and grasp the hand of the Almighty, embracing His call to partnership.

Understanding the Divine Handshake

A handshake is an act of agreement, mutual understanding, and commitment to work together. When we speak of the *Divine Handshake*, we refer to a spiritual reality where heaven and earth meet, where God extends His hand to us, inviting us to work alongside Him to fulfill His purposes on earth. This concept is not just theological; it is deeply practical and transformational. It means understanding our role as believers, knowing how to operate in the authority given to us, and recognizing that we are not merely servants of God but His co-workers and friends.

In **2 Corinthians 6:1**, Paul writes, "As God's co-workers, we urge you not to receive God's grace in vain." This verse emphasizes the divine partnership we are called to. We are co-workers with God, not passive observers. God's grace was never meant to be static; it was meant to empower us for action, to fulfill His will on earth as it is in heaven. We must understand that God's invitation is not to work *for* Him but *with* Him.

Heaven's Invitation and Our Response

The concept of an *open heaven* is crucial in understanding how to co-labor with God. When Jesus was baptized, the heavens were torn open, and the Spirit descended upon Him like a dove (**Mark 1:10**). This dramatic moment marked the beginning of a new era—a time when heaven was made accessible, and God's presence was no longer confined to a particular place or time. It was a declaration that God's kingdom had come near, and His hand was extended toward humanity, inviting us into His reality.

In **Revelation 4:1**, John describes a vision where a door stands open in heaven, and a voice says, "Come up here, and I will show you what must take place after this." This is heaven's invitation—a call to rise above our earthly perspective and see from God's vantage point. It is a call to live under an open heaven where God's presence, power, and provision are readily available. But to do so, we must change our perspective, align our hearts with His, and respond to His invitation.

The Venue of the Divine Handshake

As we explore the idea of co-laboring with God, it is essential to understand where this divine handshake takes place—the House of God. In the New Testament, the Church is described as the *ekklesia*, the assembly of believers, and the *oikos*, the household of faith. It is within this community that the divine handshake is made manifest. As living stones, we are being built into a spiritual house, offering spiritual sacrifices acceptable to God through Jesus Christ (**1 Peter 2:5**). This spiritual house is where believers are taught, challenged, and inspired to grow in revelation, faith, and action.

The strength of the Church determines the effectiveness of the divine handshake. The early Church understood this well. They devoted themselves to the apostles' teaching, fellowship, breaking of bread, and prayer (**Acts 2:42**). This devotion created an atmosphere of open heaven, where signs and wonders were commonplace, and God's presence was tangible. Today, we must return to that place of communion, community, and covenant to experience the fullness of what God has for us under an open heaven.

The Call to Reformation and Risk

Throughout history, God has called His people to co-labor with Him in bringing about reformation. Whether it was David's mighty men who were willing to be taught, challenged, and inspired (**1 Chronicles 12**) or the early Church that turned the world upside down, the catalyst for any reformation has always been a willingness to be reshaped. God is not trying to do church in the 21st century like He did in the 20th century. He calls for a fresh revelation of His Kingdom that requires risk, action, and a willingness to operate by faith.

Faith is not passive; it is dynamic. It requires stepping out of our comfort zones and embracing the unknown. As this book will explore, operating by faith will only affect your sphere of influence. Faith demands that we believe, understand, and walk in obedience, accepting God's invitation to live under an open heaven. This is the essence of the divine handshake—partnering with God in faith to see His Kingdom come on earth as it is in heaven.

The Purpose of This Book

The Divine Handshake is a journey into the heart of what it means to partner with God. It is an exploration of how heaven's invitation connects with our daily reality, how God's extended hand beckons us to live in His presence, and how we can cultivate a life that reflects His Kingdom. This book will guide you through the various dimensions of co-laboring with God—understanding the framework of the divine handshake, the venue of the handshake (the House of God), and the lifestyle that maintains an open heaven over your life.

As you read these pages, I hope you will be inspired to stretch out your hand toward the Father, just as He has stretched out His hand toward you. You will grasp His hand with intention, commitment, and a deep desire to co-labor with Him. Remember, God is not just waiting for us to do something for Him; He is inviting us to do something with Him. His hand is extended—will you take hold of it?

The divine handshake is more than just a concept; it is a call to action. It is God's invitation to step into a life of purpose, power, and partnership. Like Adam reaching out to touch the hand of God, we are called to respond to heaven's invitation with faith, courage, and expectation. May this book be a guide, a challenge, and an encouragement for you to step into the fullness of what God has for you. Under an open heaven, with His hand in yours, there is no limit to what God can do through you.

Foreword

Undoubtedly, the excitement beginning to fuel today's church involves the awakening of purpose. By His grace, God has reawakened the Body of Christ to realize the great destiny Jesus intended by which believers stand privileged to co-labor with our King. This profound reality—that we provide dreams, desires, and locations for the manifestation of God's glory on earth—is metaphorically represented in Scripture as the hand of God. It is this "divine handshake" between heaven and earth, between God and man, that is capturing the hearts and minds of believers worldwide today.

For too long, many in the church have been content to sit on the sidelines, believing that the work of bringing heaven to earth was the task of a select few—the pastors, the missionaries, the evangelists. But now, a seismic shift is occurring. The Holy Spirit is awakening us to the truth that each of us, regardless of our role or position, is called to be an active participant in God's redemptive plan. We are beginning to see that every moment of our lives, every encounter, and every opportunity can become a stage where heaven touches earth. The ordinary is becoming extraordinary because we are learning to recognize the sacred in every aspect of our lives.

My friend, Manny Rivera, comprehensively and effectively presents the theology and practical process by which every believer can experience the thrill of high-level participation with God. In these pages, Manny guides us beyond the surface of spiritual clichés and into the depths of what it means to indeed partner with God in His mission. He invites us to explore the full scope of our divine calling, providing us the tools to step out in boldness, confidence, and unwavering faith. This book handily equips Christians with the necessary confidence and intimacy to imagine and realize their business, church, school, friends, and every sphere of influence as dynamic opportunities for heaven to mingle with earth and for earth to flourish under the kindness of God.

For those who dare to dream big dreams with God, this book will be an indispensable guide. It challenges us to go beyond passive faith and invites us to embrace an active, living faith—one that constantly seeks out new ways to manifest God's Kingdom here and now. Manny offers profound insights into how we can align our desires with God's will, how we can step into our unique callings with courage, and how we can co-create with God to see His purposes fulfilled in our generation. His words remind us that we are not waiting for heaven to break through; instead, heaven is waiting for us to extend our hands in faith and take hold of God's promises.

For any believer who understands that our salvation involves more than a "ticket to heaven" and that our sonship exists to lessen earth's groaning and manifest His goodness, this is a must-read book. Manny's passion for seeing the Kingdom of God established in every corner of society is evident on every page, and his message is both timely and timeless. He writes with a conviction that challenges complacency and with a grace that invites all of us to step into the fullness of what God has prepared for us.

In this book, you will find a compelling call to action, an invitation to embrace the fullness of life as a co-laborer with Christ. It is not merely a theological discourse but a roadmap for living out the divine handshake in practical, transformative ways. As you read, you will be inspired to see your world through God's eyes and to step boldly into the partnership He offers you. Manny's words will stir your spirit, challenge your faith, and ignite a passion within you to live out the purposes of God with zeal and joy.

So, prepare your heart and mind to be stretched, challenged, and deeply encouraged. For in these pages, you will find the keys to unlocking a life of extraordinary purpose, where heaven and earth intersect in beautiful and powerful ways. You will discover what it truly means to be a partner with God in the grandest adventure of all—the unfolding of His Kingdom on earth.

Jim Hennesy
Lead Pastor of Trinity Church, Cedarhill, Texas

CHAPTER 1

The Handshake

Introduction to the Divine Handshake

The Divine Handshake is a powerful symbol of the partnership between God and us, His children. It is more than a simple gesture; it's a profound covenant, sealed by the blood of Jesus Christ, that allows heaven to intersect with earth. This partnership invites us to move beyond being mere servants of God and to step into a deeper, more intimate relationship where we become friends of God and co-laborers in His divine mission.

This isn't just an idea but a foundational truth rooted in Scripture.

2 Corinthians 6:1—"Working together with Him, then, we appeal to you not to receive the grace of God in vain."

This scripture emphasizes that we are not called to receive God's grace passively but to work alongside Him actively.

1 Corinthians 3:9—"For we are co-workers in God's service; you are God's field, God's building."

These verses reveal that we are not just passive recipients in this divine relationship but actively involved in God's work on earth.

John 15:14-15—"You are my friends if you do what I command you. I no longer call you servants, for the servant does not know what his master is doing, but I have called you friends."

This is a promotion of epic proportions. Moving from servanthood to friendship with God is the essence of the Divine Handshake. It is an invitation into a new level of relationship where we share in the heart of God, understand His desires, and align our lives with His purpose.
The Divine Handshake is about more than just understanding a theological concept. It is about living in a way that aligns heaven with earth, where every action, decision, and thought partners with God's will.

The Restoration of Heaven on Earth

The Divine Handshake is also about the restoration of heaven on earth. Let's return to the beginning—to the Garden of Eden, where heaven and earth existed in perfect harmony. There was a time when God walked with humanity, where the boundaries between the divine and the earthly were seamless. Yet, through sin, we lost that direct connection. Heaven and earth were separated.

But since the resurrection, God has extended His hand to us once again, giving us the opportunity to bring heaven to earth. Heaven was lost in the Garden, but it is regained through Christ. This is what Jesus accomplished. Through His life, death, and resurrection, He bridged the gap that sin had created. Jesus became the propitiation for our sins, the mediator between God and man. At His resurrection, He didn't just conquer death, hell, and the grave; He restored access to heaven.

Hebrews 4:16—"Let us then approach God's throne of grace with confidence, so that we may receive mercy and find grace to help us in our time of need."

Because of the Divine Handshake, we have direct access to God's throne. And this is what we pray for every time we recite the Lord's Prayer:

Matthew 6:10—"Your kingdom come, you will be done, on earth as it is in heaven."

This is not a mere recitation; it is a call to action, an invitation to bring the reality of heaven to every corner of the earth.

Picture Michelangelo's famous painting on the ceiling of the Sistine Chapel. You know the one—where Adam reaches out his finger, and God is reaching back. The fingers are so close, but they don't quite touch. It's a powerful image, but I think it stops short. Michelangelo understood the concept of humanity meeting divinity, but I believe it's not just about touch. I believe it's a handshake.

A handshake represents agreement, trust, and a shared commitment. The Divine Handshake isn't just about touching God's fingertips; it's about grasping His hand and agreeing to partner with Him in bringing His kingdom to earth. It's not a distant, casual connection. It's intimate, committed, and covenantal. Because of this divine handshake, we now have access to everything that Jesus has.

From Servants to Friends: A Divine Promotion

Let's discuss what it means to move from being servants to becoming friends of God. In ancient times, a servant, or "Doulos" in Greek, was someone bound to serve their master. They didn't have the privilege of understanding the master's heart or intentions; they followed orders. But Jesus, in His radical love, changes the dynamic entirely.

John 15:14-15—"You are my friends if you do what I command you. No longer do I call you servants, for the servant does not know what his master is doing, but I have called you friends."

This shift from "doulos" (servant) to "philos" (friend) profoundly transforms our relationship with God.

A servant might obey out of fear or obligation, but a friend obeys out of love and relationship. Friends of God have access to His heart. We don't just follow commands; we understand the reasons behind them. It's like considering the difference between an employee and a business partner. An employee might do the job because they have to, but a business partner is invested in the vision and mission of the company. Similarly, as friends of God, we are invested in His heart and His mission for the world.

Friends are less concerned about disobeying and more focused on not disappointing. This is the heart of the Divine Handshake. When we are in a friendship with God, our motivation shifts from just "doing what is right" to wanting to please Him because of our love. There is a deeper intimacy, a greater trust, and a more profound connection.

But this transition isn't automatic. We can't jump from being distant to being friends without first understanding what it means to be a servant. Before we can ever be friends of God, we must first learn what it means to be His servants. Servanthood is where we learn obedience, humility, and faithfulness. A faithful servant is a "bond slave," someone who willingly gives themselves up to another's will. It's not about punching in a time clock; it's about giving our lives entirely to the prosperity of our Master's estate.

The Divine Handshake: A Partnership with God

The Divine Handshake is not a distant touch but a committed partnership. It's not just being in God's proximity but engaging in a meaningful partnership where heaven invades earth through our lives. Think of it like this: when Jesus extends His hand, it's not just a gesture; it's a covenant. A handshake is an agreement, and through this Divine Handshake, we have access to everything that Jesus has.

We see this concept throughout the Scriptures.

1 Corinthians 3:9—"For we are co-workers in God's service; you are God's field, God's building."

When Paul speaks about being "co-workers in God's service," he talks about more than just performing tasks. He's talking about sharing in

God's heart and God's mission. We are not working for Him; we are working from Him. It's a partnership where we align our will with His and become conduits for His presence in the world.

This idea of partnership means we are not passive observers but active participants in God's work. It's not about waiting for heaven to come down; it's about bringing heaven to earth through our lives. We are called to be His hands and feet, to carry His presence into every situation, every circumstance, every encounter.

Paradigm Shifts in Our Relationship with God

To fully embrace the Divine Handshake, several paradigm shifts must take place within us. These shifts are essential to understanding who we are in God and how we are to live out this divine partnership.

Paradigm Shift 1: What We Know is Altered

Romans 12:2—"Do not conform to the pattern of this world, but be transformed by renewing your mind."

This is the first paradigm shift—our understanding of reality changes when we enter a divine partnership with God. No longer are we bound by the limitations of our human perspective; we gain access to God's wisdom and knowledge.

We start to see things differently. The truths of God's Word become the foundation for how we see the world. Some of us may have turned our worlds upside down as we read the Word and encountered new revelations that challenge our previous understanding. That's a good thing! When God shakes our experience, He's making room for a greater revelation. It's in this place of shaking that freedom begins to emerge.

When our knowledge is altered, we begin to see possibilities where there were once impossibilities. We start to understand that with God, all things are possible.

Matthew 19:26—"With man this is impossible, but with God all things are possible."

This shift in understanding is crucial because it sets the foundation for how we live, pray, and interact with the world around us.

Paradigm Shift 2: Our Experiences Change

Encountering God as a friend rather than merely a servant transforms our experiences. It changes the way we interact with Him, the way we pray, and the way we live. The book of Acts gives us a powerful example of this.

Acts 2:1-4—"When the day of Pentecost came, they were all together in one place. Suddenly, a sound like the blowing of a violent wind came from heaven and filled the whole house where they were sitting. They saw what seemed to be tongues of fire that separated and came to rest on each of them. All of them were filled with the Holy Spirit and began to speak in other tongues as the Spirit enabled them."

This was a game-changer. This wasn't just an isolated event but a new way of living—a life empowered by the Spirit.

I remember a story about a housewife who was so hungry for a baptism of the Holy Spirit that she started cleaning her oven. She felt drawn to get into the back of the oven, scrubbing, praying, and asking God to baptize her with His Spirit. And right there, as she was on her knees, the power of God hit her, and she began to speak in tongues. She wasn't in a church. She wasn't at an altar. She was in her kitchen, cleaning her oven, and she encountered the living God.

Our encounters with God don't have to be confined to church settings. They can happen anywhere—at home, in the car, at work—because the Divine Handshake means heaven is always accessible. When we embrace this partnership, His heartbeat becomes our heartbeat. Revival begins in the hearts of those who have had a genuine encounter with God, and these experiences become the catalyst for transformation.

Paradigm Shift 3: Our Function in Life is Revised

Ephesians 2:10—"For we are God's handiwork, created in Christ Jesus to do good works, which God prepared in advance for us to do."

In the kingdom of God, function isn't defined by what we do but by why we do it. When we understand our divine partnership with God, our function in life becomes clear: we are called to bring His kingdom to earth.

This shift requires us to move from a mindset of performance to one of purpose. We are no longer motivated by the need to earn God's approval but by a desire to fulfill His will. Whether we are preaching from the pulpit, running a business, or taking care of our families, our function is to reflect the character and nature of God in all we do. It's about more than just doing tasks for God; it's about living from the heart of God.

God entrusts us with more of His power when our function is revised. As we shift from merely doing tasks for God to working with God, He entrusts us with greater responsibility and authority. This is what it means to walk in the Divine Handshake: partnering with God so His power flows through us to impact the world.

Paradigm Shift 4: Our Identity is Transformed

Galatians 2:20—"I have been crucified with Christ and I no longer live, but Christ lives in me."

Our identity as friends of God transforms everything about us. We no longer live for ourselves; we live for Christ. This is the ultimate paradigm shift—understanding that our worth and purpose are found not in what we do but in who we are in Him.

When our identity is transformed, we are no longer swayed by the opinions or expectations of others. We live from the revelation of who the Father says we are. This freedom allows us to walk confidently in our calling, knowing that God fully accepts and loves us.

Our new identity as friends of God also means that we have access to His resources, wisdom, and power. We are not just servants following orders but partners in His mission to redeem the world. This transformation in identity is the foundation for living out the Divine Handshake, as it empowers us to move beyond fear and into faith.

Living Out the Divine Handshake: Practical Applications

The Divine Handshake is more than a concept; it's a lifestyle. To live it out, we must take practical steps to align our lives with this divine partnership.

Engaging with God in Daily Life

The Divine Handshake invites us to walk with God daily. This means cultivating a lifestyle of prayer, worship, and studying His Word. The more we engage with God, the more we understand His heart and desires for us and the world around us. Our partnership with God becomes evident in how we treat others, handle challenges, and pursue His purposes above our own.

Real-life Testimonies: Baptism in the Holy Spirit and Personal Transformation

Testimonies are potent reminders of how God moves when we embrace the Divine Handshake. Whether it's the story of someone being baptized in the Holy Spirit while cleaning their oven or my experience of encountering God in unexpected places, these stories remind us that God meets us where we are. He responds to our hunger and our desire for Him.

Practical Steps for Embracing the Divine Handshake
1. **Seek Intimacy with God:** Spend prayer, worship, and reading the Bible daily. Make it a priority to cultivate a personal relationship with God.
2. **Serve with Joy:** Recognize that serving God is not a burden but a privilege. Serve others with the heart of a friend of God, knowing that you are working from Him, not just for Him.
3. **Stay Hungry for His Presence:** Desire more of God in every area of your life. Ask for fresh encounters with His Spirit and be open to His leading, even in unexpected places.
4. **Walk in Your New Identity:** Understand that you are a friend of God. Live boldly, knowing you have been given access to His presence, power, and purpose.

Michelangelo's Creation of Adam: A Deeper Look into the Divine Handshake

Michelangelo's *Creation of Adam* is more than just a stunning fresco; it is a profound reflection on the relationship between humanity and the divine. Painted between 1508 and 1512 on the ceiling of the Sistine Chapel, this artwork has captivated viewers for centuries. The image of God and Adam, suspended in that almost-touch, has become one of the most recognized and revered depictions of divine interaction in art history. Yet, to truly understand the depth of what Michelangelo captured and how it relates to the Divine Handshake, we must look closer at the painting's details, context, and theological implications.

The Space Between the Fingers: Potential and Promise

At the heart of *The Creation of Adam* is the narrow gap between God's outstretched finger and Adam's. This small distance holds significant meaning. God is depicted with dynamic energy—His arm is outstretched, His body is twisted with purpose, and His gaze is intensely focused on Adam. God is actively reaching out, surrounded by a host of angels, representing the full power of heaven moving toward man. In contrast, Adam's posture is passive. His hand is relaxed, and his body reclines as if waiting, almost indifferent. The space between them speaks volumes about the potential for connection and the reality of disconnection.

This space between the fingers symbolizes humanity's potential to reach out and grasp the divine. It represents the promise of a relationship, the offer of God's presence, and the proximity of His grace. But it also highlights a critical truth: God's hand is extended, but it requires action on our part to close the gap. The painting captures a moment of decision—will humanity respond to God's reach?

Divine Initiative: God's Reaching Hand

Michelangelo portrays God with an assertive, almost urgent motion, illustrating that the divine initiative is permanently active. God is not passive; He is not sitting back, waiting for us to come to Him. From the beginning, God has desired to be in a relationship with humanity. His hand always reaches out to us, inviting us into a deeper connection.

Genesis 3:9—"But the Lord God called to the man, 'Where are you?'"

Theologically, this is a powerful representation of God's relentless pursuit of humanity. God sought them out in the Garden of Eden when Adam and Eve sinned. When Israel strayed, God sent prophets to call them back. And in the ultimate act of divine initiative, God sent His Son, Jesus Christ, to bridge the gap that sin had created. In Michelangelo's fresco, this divine initiative is captured perfectly. God is reaching out with all His might, embodying the message that He is always ready to engage with us, partner with us, and offer His hand.

The Passive Hand of Adam: Human Hesitation

On the other side of the fresco, Adam's hand is depicted as almost lifeless, lacking the energy and eagerness of God's reach. Adam's body is fully formed, his muscular frame lying on the earth, yet his hand does not match the urgency of God's. This relaxed posture of Adam speaks to a common spiritual reality—human hesitation. Even when God reaches out to us, many remain passive, unsure, or indifferent.

Revelation 3:20—"Here I am! I stand at the door and knock. If anyone hears my voice and opens the door, I will come in and eat with that person, and they will be with me."

Adam's hand symbolizes humanity's hesitation to grasp God's hand fully. This limp hand represents a heart not fully engaged in the divine relationship, whether due to fear, complacency, doubt, or a lack of understanding. It's as if Michelangelo asks each of us: Are we content with being close to God without genuinely connecting with Him? Are we satisfied with being near His presence but not fully grasping it?

The Divine Handshake: Moving Beyond the Gap

Michelangelo's *Creation of Adam* gives us a profound visual metaphor for the Divine Handshake, but it stops short of the whole picture. While the painting beautifully captures the potential for connection, the Divine Handshake requires us to move beyond potential into action. It's not enough for us to reach toward God; we must grasp His hand firmly. We must move from the almost-touch to the entire grip.

The gap between God and Adam's fingers in the painting is where many of us live spiritually—close but not quite there. We sense God's presence, we feel His nearness, but we don't fully commit to the handshake. The Divine Handshake is about closing that gap, about moving beyond a passive relationship into an active, engaged partnership with God.

When discussing the Divine Handshake, we discuss a complete and committed engagement with God. It's about grasping His hand, knowing it's not a casual touch but a binding agreement. In the ancient world, a handshake was not just a greeting but a sign of agreement, a covenant sealed with intent. The Divine Handshake is sealed by the blood of Jesus, who bridged the gap between heaven and earth once and for all.

Symbolism of the Surrounding Figures:
Heaven's Witness to the Handshake

Looking beyond just the hands, we notice the figures surrounding God. Michelangelo painted God enveloped in a billowing cloak, supported by angels who seem to propel Him toward Adam. Among these figures, art historians often highlight a striking figure under God's left arm—a woman who appears to gaze directly at Adam. Some interpret this figure as Eve, not yet created in the narrative but already present in the mind of God. This detail speaks to the completeness of God's plan for humanity—a plan that includes relationship, partnership, and the Divine Handshake from the beginning.

The angels surrounding God symbolize heaven's full support for this divine-human connection. When we reach out to God, all of heaven cheers us on, encouraging us to step into our rightful place as co-laborers with God. Heaven is fully invested in this partnership, and Michelangelo captures this—the divine urgency and heavenly backing of God's desire for a relationship with humanity.

From Renaissance Art to Spiritual Reality:
Completing the Creation

Michelangelo's painting, created during the Renaissance—a period of immense rediscovery of human potential and divine relationship—illustrates a moment that captures the essence of God's desire for humanity. Yet, while *The Creation of Adam* gives us a glimpse of the divine reaching out to the human, it only captures half of the story. It captures the divine initiative but not the human response.

The Divine Handshake requires us to complete this picture. It challenges us to envision what happens after this scene—when Adam's hand reaches back with equal intensity, when humanity responds to God's reach not with passivity but with passion. We are called to engage fully in this divine partnership, not to remain on the fringes of divine grace but to dive into its depths.

Closing the Gap: A Call to Grasp the Divine Hand

When we think of the Divine Handshake, we must imagine the scene beyond what Michelangelo painted. Imagine Adam not just reaching but grasping. Imagine the gap closing, the hands meeting in a firm grip, symbolizing the full acceptance of God's invitation to partnership. The Divine Handshake is about saying "yes" to God's invitation and fully engaging with Him, just as He is fully engaged with us.

James 4:8—"Draw near to God, and He will draw near to you."

God's hand is extended, and it always has been. The question is whether we will continue to mirror Adam's hesitance or move beyond it into a place of full embrace. The Divine Handshake is not merely a moment but a lifestyle—a commitment to walk with God, to work with God, and to partner with God in bringing heaven to earth.

Theological Reflections: Beyond Renaissance Symbolism

Theologically, Michelangelo's fresco symbolizes the potential and promise inherent in our creation. It reflects the tension between divine sovereignty and human responsibility. God reaches out with everything—His creation, His redemption, His Spirit. Now, it is up to us to reach back with the same intensity, to take hold of the Divine Handshake and live in the fullness of this partnership.

Living the Divine Handshake: A Practical Invitation

As we look at Michelangelo's fresco, let it be more than just a piece of art. Let it be a reminder that God is reaching out to us with vigor and love. He is not holding back. And our response should not be one of hesitation. We are called to be more than passive observers; we are called active participants in God's divine plan. Let us close the gap. Let us take hold of the Divine Handshake with both hands, committing to this covenant of love and purpose.

Michelangelo painted a world where the potential for divine connection is ever-present. But our reality as believers is to live beyond potential—we are called to live in promise, to complete the picture that Michelangelo left open-ended. It's our turn to grasp His hand and step thoroughly into the divine partnership that changes everything.

Walking as Friends of God

The Divine Handshake is a spiritual reality that redefines our relationship with God. It moves us from servanthood to friendship, from mere obedience to intimate partnership. This is our spiritual inheritance—a life of deep connection with God, empowered by His Spirit and aligned with His purpose.

As you continue to seek God, may you fully embrace this divine partnership. May you walk as a friend of God, bringing heaven to earth wherever you go. May your life be a testimony of His love, power, and glory as you live out the anatomy of the Divine Handshake.

Let's never forget: We are not just trying to get something; we already have it. We are not trying to get there; we are already there. We are His friends. His hand is extended—grab hold of it, and let's walk in this divine partnership together.

CHAPTER 2

The Blank Checks of Friendship

The Unlimited Wish of the Divine

From our earliest years, the idea of having a wish granted captivates our imaginations. As children, many of us dreamed of encountering a magical genie, one who would offer us a single wish that could fulfill our deepest desires. Conversations with siblings and friends often centered around this: "If you had one wish, what would it be?" I remember these conversations vividly. My brother, Raul, ever the entrepreneur, even at a young age, always had a ready answer: "I'd wish for a hundred more wishes!" Of course, there were always the rules—like in Disney's *Aladdin*—that you couldn't wish for more wishes.

But what if this fantasy wasn't as far-fetched as we thought? What if there was a precedent for this, not in fairy tales but in divine reality? There is one person in biblical history who encountered something even more significant than a genie with a lamp. Solomon, son of David, was granted an extraordinary offer by God Himself: a blank check, a divine wish, a heavenly opportunity to ask for anything his heart desired.

1 Kings 3:5—"At Gibeon, the Lord appeared to Solomon during the night in a dream, and God said, 'Ask for whatever you want me to give you.'"

Solomon's request for wisdom marked a pivotal moment in biblical history. It raised the bar of what was possible in prayer and divine-human interaction. But the story didn't end with Solomon. What if I told you that Jesus, in His infinite love and grace, has given us, His followers, something even more astonishing than Solomon's wish? Not just one blank check but an endless supply of them.

Promises Rooted in Friendship

When Jesus spoke to His disciples, He wasn't merely addressing them; He was speaking to every believer who would follow. Every time the Bible mentions the disciples, it speaks to us, the New Testament believers. What Jesus offered His disciples was not a one-time gift; it was a standing invitation, an open-ended promise to all who would abide in Him and live in friendship with God. And this is where the concept of "blank checks" comes in—not a single wish, but an unlimited offering rooted in a deep, abiding relationship with the Creator of the universe.

The promises given by Jesus are not casual, nor are they to be taken lightly. They are profound, earth-shaking, heaven-moving guarantees that come with the weight of God's glory and the intimacy of His friendship. When He said, "You are my friends," He was inviting us into a relationship where nothing is withheld, where we are given access to the treasures of heaven because of our closeness to Him.

John 15:7—"If you abide in Me, and My words abide in you, you will ask what you desire, and it shall be done for you."

Notice the condition here: "If you abide in Me." This is not a mechanical formula where we plug in the right words and out pop a miracle. No, this is about abiding, dwelling, and remaining in Him. It's about living in such a way that our desires are no longer our own but are the very desires of God's heart flowing through us. When we live in that place of profound union with Christ, our "asking" becomes an extension of His will, and His will is always fulfilled.

John 15:16—"You did not choose Me, but I chose you and appointed you that you should go and bear fruit, and that your fruit should remain, that whatever you ask the Father in My name He may give you."

This is one of the many blank checks given to us. We did not initiate this relationship; God did. He chose us, He appointed us, and He desires that our lives bear fruit that lasts. It's not about fleeting moments of spiritual highs; it's about enduring impact—fruit that remains. And in this abiding friendship, we are empowered to ask boldly, knowing that whatever we ask in His name, in alignment with His character and purposes, He will give us.

John 14:14—"If you ask anything in My name, I will do it."

John 16:23-24—"And in that day you will ask Me nothing. Most assuredly, I say to you, whatever you ask the Father in My name He will give you. Until now you have asked nothing in My name. Ask, and you will receive that your joy may be full."

These promises aren't just ancient texts but living, breathing words that hold power today. For many of us, these blank checks are lying unused. We keep them in our hands but don't dare to cash them in because our view of God has been limited by our experiences, our disappointments, and our fears. Yet, Jesus is calling us to a deeper understanding. He is calling us to friendship, to partnership, to co-labor with Him in ways that defy human logic and limitations.

God Awaits Our Desires

God never intended for our relationship with Him to be mechanical or robotic. He is not looking for puppets on strings who follow commands without heart or emotion. Our God is a relational God, a Father who delights in His children. He has created us with unique desires, dreams, and aspirations, and He longs to hear them from us.

Too often, the church is waiting for the next word from God, believing that the following divine directive will set them on their path. But what if, instead, God is waiting for a word from us? What if the Father sits on the edge of His seat, waiting to hear our dreams, desires, and deepest longings?

Psalm 37:4—"Delight yourself also in the Lord, and He shall give you the desires of your heart."

This is not just about getting what we want; it is about aligning our hearts so closely with His that what we desire is what He desires. It is about living in such a way that our hearts beat in rhythm with His, that our prayers are not just requests but are conversations between intimate friends. This is the blank check of friendship—a divine invitation to dream with God.

The Depth of Co-Laboring with God

To understand the depth of this relationship, we must grasp what it means to co-labor with God. We were created to have a relationship with Him and share in His activity and authority. God's love relationship with mankind is never separate from His purpose for humanity. Our love relationship with God is never independent of the mission He has called us to fulfill. We are invited to participate in a divine dance of intimacy and purpose—a partnership where heaven meets earth through our lives.

2 Corinthians 6:1—"Working together with Him, then, we appeal to you not to receive the grace of God in vain."

Working *with* Him, not *for* Him. This subtle difference transforms everything. God doesn't desire mere workers; He desires friends who work alongside Him, carrying His presence into every sphere of life. We don't work for His approval; we work from His presence. It is not about striving to earn His favor but about flowing from His love and power that already resides within us.

Imagine this: the Creator of the universe, the King of kings, extends His hand to us, not as a master to a servant, but as a friend to a friend. This is the Divine Handshake—a covenantal agreement to partner with Him in manifesting His Kingdom on earth as it is in heaven.

The Power of Intimacy: Into-Me-See

Intimacy with God is not just an emotional experience but the foundation of effective co-laboring. True intimacy can be understood as "into-me-see"—a vulnerability and transparency where nothing is hidden. When we draw near to God in this kind of relationship, He reveals His heart, plans, and purposes. Prayer, worship, praise, and meditation on His Word are not just religious activities; they are the expressions of a vibrant, living relationship with the Father.

Genesis 28:17—"How awesome is this place! This is none other than the house of God; this is the gate of heaven."

When Jacob saw the ladder reaching heaven in his dream, he recognized that he was in a place of divine connection—a gate of heaven. In the same way, when we engage in intimacy with God, we become a living gate where heaven touches earth. Our lives become the very bridge where the will of God is enacted on earth. This is not just about receiving divine downloads but about becoming divine conduits—partners in the divine handshake.

The Divine Purpose: Source, Means, and Destiny

All movement in the universe—every act of God and every purpose of His heart—is characterized by three essential elements: a source, a means, and a destiny. These three elements are not merely philosophical ideas but are deeply rooted in the nature of God and His eternal plan for creation. Understanding these three characteristics helps us align ourselves with God's will, revealing our role in His divine narrative.

Source: The origin of all things, which is God Himself.
Means: The method or vehicle by which God's purposes are carried out.
Destiny: The end goal, the fulfillment of God's purposes on earth and in heaven.

Romans 11:36—"For from Him and through Him and to Him are all things. To Him be the glory forever."

This verse captures the essence of these three characteristics—God is the beginning, the middle, and the end of all things. He is the Alpha and the Omega, the source from which everything flows, the means by which everything is sustained, and the destiny to which everything moves. Let us unpack these three characteristics to understand their implications fully.

1. **Source: The Origin of All Things**

God is the ultimate source of all creation. Everything that exists has its beginning in Him. When we speak of God as the "Source," we speak of Him as the originator, the Creator who spoke the universe into existence out of nothing. This truth sets the foundation for all theology and understanding of purpose. Nothing exists outside of Him, and nothing has a life apart from Him.

Genesis 1:1—"In the beginning, God created the heavens and the earth."

Before there was light, time, space, or matter, there was God. He is self-existent, uncreated, and eternal. In His infinite wisdom and love, He chose to create. Creation itself is an overflow of God's nature—His love, His creativity, His power, and His desire for relationship. When we recognize God as the source, we acknowledge that everything begins with Him and must return to Him.

As the source, God implies that all things find their identity and purpose in Him. Just as a river cannot exist without its source, neither can we understand our existence apart from God. To say that God is the source is to say that He is the reason, the rationale behind everything that is. He is the author of all life, the fountain from which all wisdom, power, and love flow.

Colossians 1:16—"For in Him all things were created: things in heaven and on earth, visible and invisible, whether thrones or powers or rulers or authorities; all things have been created through Him and for Him."

This passage clarifies that all things were created through Him and for Him. He is not just the starting point but the cause behind everything. Recognizing God as our source means that we live with the understanding that every breath we take, every moment of our existence, and every ounce of our being is sustained by Him.

2. **Means: The Method or Vehicle by Which God's Purposes Are Carried Out**

If God is the source of all things, the means are how His purposes are brought to fruition. The "means" are the divine methods, the vehicles by which God's plans are executed in the temporal world. This includes His Word, His Spirit, His Church, and even His creation. God, in His sovereignty, has chosen various means through which His purposes are carried out.

Isaiah 55:11—"So is my word that goes out from my mouth: It will not return to me empty but will accomplish what I desire and achieve the purpose for which I sent it."

God's Word is one of the most potent means by which His purposes are accomplished. When He speaks, His Word carries creative power. It does not return void; it fulfills the very purpose for which it was sent. The Word of God is active, living, and dynamic. It is through His Word that the universe was created, and through His Word, His plans continue to unfold.

Another way God carries out His purposes is through His Spirit. The Holy Spirit is God's breath, the one who moves upon the waters of chaos and brings order. He is the comforter, the guide, and the empowerer of the Church. God works within us through the Holy Spirit, transforming our hearts, renewing our minds, and equipping us for every good work.

Zechariah 4:6—"Not by might nor by power, but by My Spirit,' says the Lord Almighty."

The Spirit of God is the agent of action in the earth. Where the Spirit moves, God's purposes are accomplished. This means that any endeavor, any mission, any calling that is not infused with the Spirit of God will not carry the weight of heaven. The Spirit is the means by which heaven's agenda is enacted on earth.

Furthermore, God has chosen to work through His people—the Church—to fulfill His purposes. We are His body, His hands, and His feet on the earth. God plans to use the Church to bring His kingdom to earth, preach the gospel, heal the sick, bind up the brokenhearted, and set captives free.

Ephesians 3:10—"His intent was that now, through the church, the manifold wisdom of God should be made known to the rulers and authorities in the heavenly realms."

The Church is God's chosen means of revealing His wisdom and glory to the seen and unseen realms. As His people, we are invited to partner with Him and become co-laborers in His mission. This partnership is not because God needs us but because He chooses to work with us. He invites us to see how His love, justice, mercy, and truth are displayed in the world.

3. Destiny: The End Goal, the Fulfillment of God's Purposes on Earth and in Heaven

If God is the source and the means are His methods, then destiny is the ultimate fulfillment of all His plans and purposes. "Destiny" speaks to the consummation, the end towards which all things are moving. The grand conclusion, the telos, is the point at which all creation reaches its intended purpose. The destiny of all things is God Himself—His glory revealed, His kingdom established, and His will done on earth as it is in heaven.

Revelation 21:6—"He said to me: 'It is done. I am the Alpha and the Omega, the Beginning and the End. To the thirsty I will give water without cost from the spring of the water of life.'»

God is not only the beginning but also the end. He is the destiny toward which all creation is heading. The end goal is not merely an abstract idea or a concept; it is the fullness of God's presence, the establishment of His eternal kingdom, and the restoration of all things to their original intent. It is the reconciliation of heaven and earth under the sovereign rule of Christ.

Philippians 2:10-11—"That at the name of Jesus every knee should bow, in heaven and on earth and under the earth, and every tongue acknowledge that Jesus Christ is Lord, to the glory of God the Father."

The destiny of all things is the glorification of Jesus Christ. Everything points to Him; in the end, every knee will bow and every tongue will confess that He is Lord. The ultimate purpose of all creation is to bring glory to God, declare His greatness, and live in His love and presence.

This destiny also includes the redemption and restoration of all creation. The Bible speaks of a new heaven and a new earth where there is no more death, no more pain, and no more suffering. This is the ultimate destiny of God's purposes—an eternal communion with Him where all things are made new.

Revelation 21:4—"He will wipe every tear from their eyes. There will be no more death or mourning or crying or pain, for the old order of things has passed away."

The destiny is a place where the fullness of God's character, His love, justice, holiness, and mercy, are fully realized. It is where God's plan reaches its completion, and we, His people, live in perfect harmony with Him, fulfilling the very reason for which we were created.

The Divine Handshake: Engaging in God's Purpose

Understanding God as the source, recognizing His means, and embracing His destiny leads us to a deeper engagement with the Divine Handshake. When we grasp these three characteristics, we begin to see our place in the divine story. We are not mere spectators but participants in the unfolding of God's eternal purpose.

When we acknowledge God as the source, we align ourselves with His creative power and purposes. When we operate through His means, we walk in the Spirit, empowered by His Word and His Church. And when we set our eyes on His destiny, we live with eternal perspective, knowing that everything we do is moving towards the fulfillment of God's glorious plan.

In the Divine Handshake, we are invited into this beautiful, redemptive story. We take His hand, not out of obligation but out of an understanding that we are a vital part of what God is doing in the world. We co-labor with Him, not because He needs us but because He desires us to experience the joy of fulfilling our God-given purpose alongside Him.

The Divine Incorporation of Humanity

God, in His omnipotence, could accomplish all things by Himself. He doesn't need us to fulfill His purposes, yet He chooses to involve us in His divine plan. This is both humbling and exhilarating. God has chosen to stretch out His hand toward us and say, "I want you to be a part of what I am doing. I want you to work with Me."

Ephesians 2:10—"For we are His workmanship, created in Christ Jesus for good works, which God prepared beforehand that we should walk in them."

This divine incorporation is the essence of the Divine Handshake. It's about stepping into the works that God has already prepared for us, not trying to create our path. We are His workmanship—crafted, molded, and shaped for His purposes.

The Necessity of Dependence on the Divine

For God to use us without our fallen nature corrupting His purposes, we must continually engage in the Divine Handshake. It is a place of dependence, humility, and trust. We must recognize that apart from Him, we can do nothing.

John 15:5—"I am the vine; you are the branches. If you remain in Me and I in you, you will bear much fruit; apart from Me you can do nothing."

When we understand this truth, we are delivered from self-reliance and the endless striving to prove ourselves. Instead, we rest in the reality that our only hope of fulfilling God's purpose is constant dependence on Him.

Embracing the Divine Handshake
God's hand is extended toward us, always inviting us to partner in His work. The Divine Handshake is not just a concept but a living reality. It's an invitation to move from servanthood to friendship, from working *for* God to working *with* God. It is about reaching out, taking hold of His hand, and allowing Him to lead us in the fullness of His purpose.

God does not waste a crisis or a valley; He uses them to bring us to a place where we reach out to Him. His hand is always extended. All we have to do is take hold and walk with Him, not just for our salvation but for the execution of His purpose on earth.

James 4:8—"Draw near to God, and He will draw near to you."

This is the essence of the Divine Handshake—drawing near, engaging in intimacy, and partnering with the Creator to bring His Kingdom to earth as it is in heaven. Reach out today, take His hand, and walk in this divine partnership with confidence and boldness.

Matthew 6:10—"Your kingdom come, Your will be done, on earth as it is in heaven."

This is the blank check of friendship. Let's cash it in.

CHAPTER 3

The Desires of Our Heart

In the life of the believer, the Holy Spirit is constantly bringing us to a place of inspiration, where He breathes in us His word. This inspiration is designed to catalyze transformation, and that transformation will ultimately bring about a powerful manifestation. As you continue to read this book, you're not just reading words; you're hearing the voice of the Holy Spirit speaking a word within this word—breathing life into your heart and setting you on a path where God's desires become your desires.

2 Corinthians 6:1—"We appeal to you not to receive the grace of God in vain. Working together with Him."

1 Corinthians 3:9—"For we are co-workers in God's service."

To be in co-mission with God is more than sharing in His mission; it is about being so aligned with His heart that His desires become our desires. We can only co-labor with Him if we understand what it means to live in submission to Him. Co-mission without submission is merely ambition. To truly work with God, we must first learn how to live *under* Him.

Since the resurrection, God has extended His hand to humanity, inviting us to partner with Him in bringing heaven to earth. We are now the house of God, the gate of heaven. His mighty hand—His presence, His essence—is extended to us in the form of a covenant.

When I talk about the Divine Handshake, I'm speaking of a sacred agreement, a spiritual partnership where His scarred hands meet ours in an eternal bond.

Matthew 6:9-10—"Our Father who art in heaven, hallowed be Thy name. Thy kingdom come, Thy will be done, on earth as it is in heaven."

Heaven is not merely a distant location; it is the very presence of God. And this presence, this heavenly realm, is not something we are meant to wait for—it is something we are called to manifest here and now. When we understand our role as co-laborers with Him, we begin to see the power of His presence, His Divine Handshake, active in our lives. Darkness must flee when we grasp this revelation because we carry the authority of His heavenly mandate within us.

Delighting in the Father: The Key to Answered Prayers
Psalm 37:4—"Delight yourself also in the Lord, and He will give you the desires of your heart."

To co-labor with Him is to reach a place where we are in deep delight with the Father, living in a realm where prayers are answered not occasionally but constantly. The word "delight" in Hebrew is *anag*, which means "to be happy about," "to take exquisite delight," or "to make merry over." This delight is not a superficial joy but a profound, soul-satisfying joy that springs from intimate fellowship with the Father.

At the beginning of creation, God's Spirit hovered over the face of the deep. And today, He is still hovering—bringing order out of chaos, speaking light into darkness, and making beauty from ashes. His presence, the Spirit of God, is like a divine parenthese in both time and space, embracing us with His ever-present proximity.

Panim: The Multidimensional Presence of God

The Hebrew word **Panim** captures the essence of God's ever-present reality. Translated often as "face" or "presence," *Panim* is a plural term in Hebrew, reflecting the layers and dimensions of God's nearness. Unlike our linear perspective of time and space, God exists in what we can call the "eternal now"—the divine ability to be fully present in every moment, both the split second before and the split second after.

Psalm 139:4-5—"Before a word is on my tongue you, Lord, know it completely. You hem me in behind and before, and you lay your hand upon me."

This scripture encapsulates the *Panim* of God in both time and space. God's presence is not just near; it surrounds us, hems us in, and guides us. His *Panim* means He is both "behind and before" us, offering a divine embrace that covers our past, leads our present, and secures our future. It means that God's presence is always "hovering"—actively engaging with us, much like it did in the beginning over the waters of creation. This is the very presence that aligns us with His heart and His desires.

Desires Shaped in the Presence of Panim

The deeper our relationship with God, the more our desires are shaped in the light of His *Panim*. When we live in constant awareness of His face turned toward us, our desires start to reflect His desires. When exposed to His presence, we find that our deepest longings transform into vehicles for His will and purposes on earth.

Psalm 27:8—"My heart says of you, 'Seek His face!' Your face, Lord, I will seek."

To seek the *Panim* of God is to desire more than just His blessings or His gifts; it is to desire Him—His face, His presence, His heart. It is to live in such a way that every breath, every action, and every decision is done with His face in view. And in this continual seeking, we find that our desires are purified, aligned, and empowered by His divine purposes.

When we engage with God's *Panim*, we are brought into His eternal perspective. Time no longer limits us, space no longer confines us, and our desires are no longer driven by earthly limitations. Instead, they are shaped by His infinite possibilities and His eternal purposes.

The Transformation of Desire: From the Father, By the Father

A profound truth lies in the understanding that our desires are deeply connected to the presence we keep. The word "desire" can be broken down into *de* (of) and *sire* (father). In its most profound sense, desire is "of the Father." The desires of our heart, when aligned with His *Panim*, are born out of fellowship with Him. They are not commanded by Him; they flow naturally from our communion with Him.

But the opposite is also true. If we spend time pondering offenses or harboring bitterness, we commune not with the Father but with the Father of lies. In that fellowship, our desires can become twisted, shaped by wounds rather than healed by His presence. When we choose to live in God's *Panim*, however, our desires are shaped for eternity. We begin to desire what He desires. The children formed in our hearts are born not of bitterness but of intimacy with the Truth.

Proverbs 13:12—"Hope deferred makes the heart sick, but a desire fulfilled is a tree of life."

This proverb, written by Solomon, brings us back to the core of God's intent for our desires. Fulfilled desires, those that align with God's will, are a tree of life—a source of divine wisdom, joy, and eternal perspective. When we are in His *Panim*, every fulfilled desire brings us deeper into His purposes, deeper into the life He intends for us.

Surrender and Transformation: The Path to Reigning with Christ

The process of surrender and personal transformation is not a mere requirement; it is the training ground for reigning with Christ forever. As we surrender to God's will, as we are transformed into His likeness, our desires begin to align with His, and those desires become a tree of life—a source of divine wisdom, joy, and eternal fulfillment.

John 16:24—"Until now you have asked nothing in My name. Ask, and you will receive that your joy may be full."

This is the life we are called to—a life of joy, peace, and fulfillment amid trials and tribulations. Jesus Himself walked this path. He lived with the joy set before Him, enduring the cross because He knew the Father's will and walked in constant fellowship with Him.

Panim and the Fulfillment of Desires: An Invitation to Intimacy and Manifestation

The concept of *Panim* invites us into a continuous dance with God's presence. It calls us to live face-to-face with Him, not as a distant God but as a God whose face shines upon us, whose presence is with us in every moment. In this closeness, our desires are refined, purified, and directed toward His divine will.

When we live in His *Panim*, the desires of our hearts are no longer our own; they are His. And when our desires align with Him, they come with the full backing of heaven. Every prayer becomes a declaration, every dream becomes a prophecy, and every desire becomes a manifestation of His kingdom on earth as it is in heaven.

Living in the Light of His Panim: The Call to Reflect His Glory

When we live in the light of God's *Panim*, we become carriers of His glory. Just as Moses' face shone after he had been with God, so too does our countenance change when we live in God's presence. The world around us will see and feel the difference. The *Panim* of God becomes the light that guides us, the warmth that comforts us, and the power that encourages us.

2 Corinthians 3:18—"And we all, who with unveiled faces contemplate the Lord's glory, are being transformed into His image with ever-increasing glory, which comes from the Lord, who is the Spirit."

This transformation is a result of living in the presence of *Panim*. As we behold Him, we are changed from glory to glory. Our desires, once self-centered, become God-centered, and in that alignment, we find the fulfillment that every human heart longs for.

Embracing the Fullness of Panim

The word *Panim* is more than a theological concept—it is a call to a relationship where we live in the fullness of God's presence. It is an invitation to dwell in His presence, to seek His face continually, and to be transformed by His glory. In His *Panim*, we find our desires aligned with His, and every aligned desire becomes a reality, a tree of life, a manifestation of heaven on earth.

This is the essence of the Divine Handshake. This is the life of fulfilled desires—a life lived in the light of His *Panim*. May we seek His face, live in His presence, and see His kingdom come through every desire of our hearts aligned with His. Amen.

This expanded chapter incorporates the concept of *Panim* directly into the theme of desires, showing how our alignment with God's presence shapes and fulfills the desires of our hearts. Let me know if there's anything you'd like further adjusted or expanded!

The Divine Handshake: A Covenant of Co-Laboring with God

The term **Divine Handshake** is a metaphor for the profound partnership and relationship that God offers to humanity. It signifies a momentary agreement and an eternal covenant between the Creator and His creation. This handshake is extended to us through the sacrifice of Jesus Christ, who bridged the chasm of sin that separated humanity from God. Through His life, death, and resurrection, the hand of God reaches out to us, inviting us into a relationship that goes beyond servanthood into the realms of friendship, co-laboring, and shared purpose.

2 Corinthians 5:20—"We are therefore Christ's ambassadors, as though God were making His appeal through us."

When discussing the Divine Handshake, we talk about something more than a symbolic gesture. It is an act of God's sovereignty and grace, reaching down to humanity with an open invitation to participate in His divine plan. It's a handshake that seals a covenant, calling us to be active participants, not passive observers, in the unfolding of His Kingdom on earth. This covenantal relationship is marked by both responsibility and intimacy—two sides of the same coin, that is, the Divine Handshake.

The Handshake as a Covenant

In ancient cultures, a handshake was not just a casual greeting. It was a sign of a covenant—an agreement that bound two parties together in purpose, trust, and mutual commitment. Similarly, the Divine Handshake signifies God's desire to enter into a covenantal relationship with us. This covenant is based on His love, sealed by the blood of Jesus and empowered by the Holy Spirit.

Genesis 15:17-18—"When the sun had set, and darkness had fallen, a smoking firepot with a blazing torch appeared and passed between the pieces. On that day, the Lord made a covenant with Abram."

In the story of Abraham, God made a covenant that involved a profound ritual, symbolizing His commitment and promise. The Divine Handshake is a continuation of this idea—God's hand extended toward us, offering a relationship that involves both promise and responsibility. Just as Abraham's covenant required faith and obedience, so did our handshake with God. It's an invitation to trust Him fully, to walk in His ways, and to participate in His redemptive work on the earth.

The Divine Handshake and Intimacy with God

The Divine Handshake is also a call to intimacy. It is not merely a contract to fulfill tasks; it is an invitation to know God deeply and to be known by Him. This handshake brings us from the status of servants to that of friends and co-laborers.

John 15:15—"I no longer call you servants because a servant does not know his master's business. Instead, I have called you friends, for everything I learned from my Father I have made known to you."

Friendship with God is the essence of the Divine Handshake. This relationship moves beyond mere obedience to a place of mutual trust, where God reveals His heart, His desires, and His plans to us. It's an intimacy where we are not just following orders but are actively engaging with God's heart and purposes. This friendship is characterized by a divine exchange where we receive the wisdom, love, and authority of God, and we, in turn, offer our obedience, love, and commitment.

Co-Laboring with God: The Partnership of the Divine Handshake

When we accept the Divine Handshake, we are agreeing to co-labor with God. This concept of co-laboring is central to the Divine Handshake. It speaks of a partnership where God involves us in His work, giving us authority and responsibility to bring His Kingdom to earth.

God does not need us to accomplish His plans, but He chooses to work through us to involve us in His divine purposes.

1 Corinthians 3:9—"For we are co-workers in God's service; you are God's field, God's building."

The beauty of the Divine Handshake is that it is not a one-sided agreement. It's not just God doing everything while we passively receive. It's an active partnership where we participate in His mission. We are His hands and feet on the earth, His ambassadors, and His voice to the nations. In this partnership, we are empowered by the Holy Spirit, guided by His Word, and driven by His love.

Matthew 28:18-20—"Then Jesus came to them and said, 'All authority in heaven and on earth has been given to me. Therefore, go and make disciples of all nations… And surely I am with you always, to the very end of the age.'»

Here, Jesus commissions His disciples to go out into the world and make disciples. This is the essence of the Divine Handshake—a shared mission where His authority is transferred to us, and we are sent out to extend His Kingdom. This co-missioning is an extension of His authority, presence, and power, allowing us to function as His representatives on earth.

The Divine Handshake and the Power of Agreement
The Divine Handshake also represents the power of agreement between God and humanity. It is about aligning our hearts, minds, and actions with His will. When we enter into this handshake with God, we are saying, "Yes, Lord, Your Kingdom come, Your will be done." It is an agreement that involves aligning our desires with His desires, our plans with His plans, and our purposes with His purposes.

Amos 3:3—"Do two walk together unless they have agreed to do so?"

For the Divine Handshake to be effective, there must be agreement. We cannot walk with God unless we agree with His direction. This requires a yielding of our own will, a surrender of our plans, and a commitment to His ways. It's not a passive surrender but an active pursuit of His heart. When we align ourselves with God's will, we enter into the flow of His purposes, and we see His Kingdom manifest on earth.

Manifesting Heaven on Earth Through the Divine Handshake

The Divine Handshake is how heaven comes to earth. When we enter into this covenant with God, we become conduits through which His presence, power, and glory are manifested in the natural realm. This is not about waiting for heaven after we die; it's about bringing heaven to earth now through our partnership with God.

Matthew 6:10—"Your kingdom come, Your will be done, on earth as it is in heaven."

When we engage in the Divine Handshake, we are agreeing to be the vessels through which God's will is done on earth as it is in heaven. We are agreeing to be the carriers of His presence, the executors of His plans, and the ambassadors of His Kingdom. This means that we live in a way that reflects heaven's reality—walking in love, justice, peace, and power. It means that we pray with authority, speak with boldness, and act with compassion.

The Divine Handshake as a Call to Faith and Action

The Divine Handshake is not just a theological concept; it's a call to faith and action. It requires us to step out boldly, take risks, and trust God in ways challenging our comfort zones. When we accept the

Divine Handshake, we are stepping into a realm where the impossible becomes possible because we are walking hand in hand with the God of the impossible.

Hebrews 11:6—"And without faith, it is impossible to please God because anyone who comes to him must believe that he exists and that he rewards those who earnestly seek him."

Faith is the currency of the Kingdom, and the Divine Handshake is the transaction where our faith meets His faithfulness. It's where our trust in Him is met with His unwavering commitment to fulfill His promises. This handshake is an act of faith, where we say, "God, I trust You. I believe in Your promises. I am willing to step out and co-labor with You in faith."

The Divine Handshake and the Role of the Holy Spirit
The Holy Spirit plays a crucial role in the Divine Handshake. He is the power and presence of God that enables us to fulfill our part of the covenant. He is the one who empowers us, equips us, and guides us as we co-labor with God. The Holy Spirit is the one who makes the impossible possible, who breathes life into our efforts, and who ensures that what we do in partnership with God bears eternal fruit.

Acts 1:8—"But you will receive power when the Holy Spirit comes on you; and you will be my witnesses in Jerusalem, and in all Judea and Samaria, and to the ends of the earth."

The Divine Handshake cannot be lived out apart from the empowerment of the Holy Spirit. He is the one who fills us with boldness, who gives us wisdom, and who anoints us for the work of the Kingdom. Without the Holy Spirit, we are merely human; with the Holy Spirit, we become divine partners in God's eternal plan.

Living Out the Divine Handshake: Practical Implications

Living in the Divine Handshake requires us to be intentional about our relationship with God. It involves daily communion with Him, seeking His face, and aligning our hearts with His. It involves stepping out in faith, trusting that His hand is guiding us, and knowing that He is with us in every endeavor.

1. **Daily Surrender**: Entering into the Divine Handshake means surrendering our will daily. It means laying down our agendas and picking up His. It's a daily decision to say, "Not my will, but Yours be done."
2. **Active Participation**: The Divine Handshake is a call to action. It means that we don't just sit back and wait for God to move; we step out in faith, knowing that He moves through us. It's about being His hands and feet, His voice and heart to the world.
3. **Alignment with His Word**: To live in the Divine Handshake, we must know His Word and live by it. His Word reveals His heart, His desires, and His plans. As we align ourselves with His Word, we align ourselves with His will.
4. **Walking in Authority**: The Divine Handshake gives us authority to bring heaven to earth. This means praying boldly, declaring His promises, and standing in faith. It means understanding the authority we have as His children and using it to push back the darkness and establish His Kingdom.

The Eternal Significance of the Divine Handshake

The Divine Handshake is God's invitation to us to enter into a relationship of covenant, intimacy, and partnership. It's a call to walk hand in hand with Him, to know His heart, to co-labor with Him, and to see His Kingdom come on earth as it is in heaven. It's a call to live in the fullness of His presence, to align our desires with His, and to manifest His glory in the world.

This handshake is not just a moment in time; it's an eternal agreement that binds us to Him forever. It's a commitment to live as His ambassadors, His co-laborers, and His friends. May we reach out and take His hand, fully embracing the Divine Handshake, and live in the fullness of all that it represents. Amen.

CHAPTER 4

Co-laboring Requires Alignment

Let's expand on the concept of **"Co-Laboring with God"** to provide a deeper understanding of this profound spiritual partnership. This expansion will explore the theological foundation of co-laboring, its biblical examples, the role of the Holy Spirit, the practical implications for believers, and the transformative power it brings to our daily walk with God.

Co-Laboring with God: A Divine Partnership

The idea of **co-laboring with God** is a cornerstone of the Christian life. It signifies a partnership where God and humanity work together to fulfill His divine purposes on earth. Co-laboring is not about working *for* God in the sense of merely carrying out tasks; it is about working *with* God and participating in His ongoing work of redemption, restoration, and renewal. This concept emphasizes our active role in God's mission and invites us to engage deeply in His Kingdom's work.

1 Corinthians 3:9—"For we are co-workers in God's service; you are God's field, God's building."

The term "co-workers" implies collaboration, joint effort, and shared responsibility. It is a powerful reminder that God has chosen to involve us in His work. Rather than acting alone, He extends an invitation to humanity to be His partners in the grand narrative of salvation. This partnership is rooted in love, founded on grace, and empowered by the Holy Spirit.

The Biblical Foundation of Co-Laboring

The concept of co-laboring with God is woven throughout Scripture, beginning with the creation narrative. From the very beginning, God created humanity not just to exist but to participate in His work. Adam and Eve were placed in the Garden of Eden to "tend and keep it" (Genesis 2:15). This mandate was an invitation to co-labor with God in stewarding creation. They were not mere spectators in God's creative process; they were active participants.

Genesis 2:15—"The Lord God took the man and put him in the Garden of Eden to work it and take care of it."

This foundational principle of co-laboring is evident in many other biblical stories:

- **Noah** was called to co-labor with God in building the ark, which became the vehicle for salvation during the flood (Genesis 6:14-22).
- **Moses** co-labored with God in leading the Israelites out of Egypt and toward the Promised Land. He was given the Ten Commandments and the plans for the Tabernacle, tasks that required human effort aligned with divine guidance (Exodus 19-31).
- **David** co-labored with God in establishing the kingdom of Israel, expanding its borders, and writing many of the Psalms that shape our worship even today.
- **The Prophets** co-labored by speaking God's truth to power, challenging the status quo, and calling the people of Israel back to covenant faithfulness.
- **The Apostles** in the New Testament were sent out as co-laborers to spread the gospel, plant churches, and build up the body of Christ through teaching, miracles, and pastoral care (Acts 1-28).

In all these examples, God provided the vision, power, and resources, but the human response of obedience, faith, and action brought God's plans to fulfillment. Co-laboring requires a deep trust in God and a willingness to step out in faith, even when the path is uncertain.

The Role of the Holy Spirit in Co-Laboring

Co-laboring with God is only possible through the empowerment of the Holy Spirit. The Holy Spirit is the one who equips, guides, and empowers us to fulfill our role as co-laborers. He is the divine enabler who works in and through us to accomplish God's purposes.

Acts 1:8—"But you will receive power when the Holy Spirit comes on you; and you will be my witnesses in Jerusalem, and in all Judea and Samaria, and to the ends of the earth."

The early church's entire mission was dependent on the power of the Holy Spirit. When Jesus ascended to heaven, He promised the disciples that the Holy Spirit would come and empower them for the task ahead. The Spirit's power was not just for miraculous signs; it was for daily living, for preaching with boldness, for loving with purity, and for serving with humility. Without the Holy Spirit, co-laboring with God would be an impossible task.

Understanding Our Role as Co-Laborers

To be a co-laborer means to partner with God in the work He is already doing. It's about aligning ourselves with His agenda, His purposes, and His ways. It requires us to listen to His voice, to be sensitive to His leading, and to be obedient to His commands. Co-laboring with God involves several key elements:

1. **Alignment with God's Vision and Will**

To co-labor with God, we must first align ourselves with His vision and will. This involves understanding God's heart and purposes for the world and for our lives. It means surrendering our plans and desires to Him and allowing Him to shape our priorities.

Romans 12:2—"Do not conform to the pattern of this world, but be transformed by the renewing of your mind. Then you will be able to test and approve what God's will is—His good, pleasing, and perfect will."

Aligning with God's will is not a one-time event; it is a daily commitment to seek His face, study His Word, and listen to His Spirit. It requires a heart posture of humility and a willingness to be led by Him, even when it challenges our comfort zones or preconceived notions.

2. **Obedience and Action**

Co-laboring with God involves not just hearing His voice but acting upon it. It requires obedience, which is often the key that unlocks God's power and presence in our lives. A call to action always accompanies God's call to co-labor with Him. When God spoke to Moses through the burning bush, it was not just to give him a revelation; it was to send him back to Egypt to deliver His people (Exodus 3).

James 2:17—"In the same way, faith by itself, if it is not accompanied by action, is dead."

Obedience is faith in action. It is the tangible expression of our trust in God. Co-laboring with God means being willing to step out in faith, even when we don't have all the answers. It's about taking that first step, trusting that God will provide what we need as we move forward.

3. Dependence on God's Strength

While co-laboring with God involves action, it also requires dependence on His strength. We are not called to do God's work in our own power. Jesus said, "Apart from me, you can do nothing" (John 15:5). True co-laboring recognizes that all fruitfulness comes from abiding in Him.

Philippians 4:13—"I can do all things through Christ who strengthens me."

Dependence on God's strength means that we acknowledge our own limitations and lean wholly on His sufficiency. It is not about striving in our flesh but about surrendering to His Spirit. When we rely on His strength, our efforts are multiplied, our burdens are lightened, and our impact is maximized.

4. Walking in Spiritual Authority

Co-laboring with God also involves walking in the spiritual authority that He has given us. When we enter into a partnership with God, we are not powerless; we are given authority to bind and loose, to heal and deliver, to preach and prophesy. This authority comes from our identity as children of God and co-heirs with Christ.

Luke 10:19—"I have given you authority to trample on snakes and scorpions and to overcome all the power of the enemy; nothing will harm you."

Walking in spiritual authority means that we operate from a place of confidence in who God is and who we are in Him. It means that we do not shrink back in fear but move forward in faith, knowing that God has empowered us to carry out His mission.

5. Co-laboring in Prayer and Intercession

Prayer is one of the most potent ways we co-labor with God. It is through prayer that we partner with God in bringing His Kingdom to earth. In prayer, we align our hearts with His, seek His will, and declare His promises. Prayer is not just a monologue; it is a dialogue with God where we listen for His voice and intercede on behalf of others.

Ezekiel 22:30—"I looked for someone among them who would build up the wall and stand before me in the gap on behalf of the land so I would not have to destroy it, but I found no one."

God is looking for those who will stand in the gap—who will co-labor with Him in prayer and intercession. This type of co-laboring requires persistence, faith, and a deep understanding of God's heart for His people.

The Transformative Power of Co-Laboring with God

When we co-labor with God, our lives are transformed. We move from being passive recipients of God's grace to active participants in His mission. This shift changes everything—our perspective, our purpose, our priorities, and our potential.

1. **Transformation of Perspective**

When we co-labor with God, we begin to see the world through His eyes. Our perspective shifts from a self-centered focus to a Kingdom-centered focus. We start to see people as God sees them, with compassion, love, and purpose. We begin to see challenges as opportunities for God to demonstrate His power and glory.

2. **Transformation of Purpose**

Co-laboring with God gives us a sense of divine purpose. We are no longer wandering aimlessly; we are walking with God in His plans and purposes. Our lives take on new meaning as we engage in His mission, whether in our workplaces, families, communities, or churches.

3. Transformation of Priorities

When we co-labor with God, our priorities are aligned with His. What matters to God becomes what matters to us. We begin to prioritize prayer, worship, service, and mission. We invest our time, talents, and resources in things that have eternal value.

4. Transformation of Potential

Finally, co-laboring with God unleashes our potential. When we partner with God, we tap into His limitless resources, wisdom, and power. We begin to operate in the gifts and callings He has placed within us, and we see His supernatural power at work in our lives.

Embracing the Call to Co-Labor

Co-laboring with God is both a privilege and a responsibility. It is an invitation to step into a divine partnership where we work alongside the Creator of the universe to bring His Kingdom to earth. It is a call to action, a call to faith, and a call to intimacy with God. It is a journey of transformation where we become more like Him as we engage in His work.

May we embrace this call with joy, humility, and faith, knowing that as we co-labor with God, we are participating in something far more significant than ourselves. We are joining with Him in the grand narrative of redemption, restoration, and renewal—a narrative that has the power to change the world. Amen.

This expanded section provides a thorough exploration of co-laboring with God, focusing on its biblical foundation, the role of the Holy Spirit, practical implications, and transformative power. Let me know if you'd like any more details or further expansion on specific points!

Alignment

Alignment with God is foundational to our spiritual journey, influencing every aspect of our relationship with Him and our ability to effectively co-labor in His purposes. This expansion will cover the meaning of alignment, its biblical foundation, how alignment affects our relationship with God, the role of the Holy Spirit, practical steps for aligning with God, and the transformational impact it has on our lives.

Alignment with God: Walking in Harmony with His Will

Alignment with God refers to the process of bringing our hearts, minds, desires, and actions into harmony with God's will, purpose, and character. It is about synchronizing our lives with His divine plan and yielding to His authority. Alignment is not just a one-time decision; it is an ongoing, daily posture of surrender and obedience. It is the intentional pursuit of God's heart and His ways, allowing His Word to shape our values, decisions, and actions.

Alignment with God means that our lives are in sync with His rhythm and direction. When we are aligned with God, His thoughts become our thoughts, His desires become our desires, and His purposes become our purposes. It is the foundation of effective co-laboring with God because we cannot partner with Him if we are not moving in the same direction.

The Biblical Foundation of Alignment with God

Alignment with God is a theme that runs throughout Scripture. From Genesis to Revelation, we see a continuous call for God's people to align themselves with His ways and purposes. Alignment is foundational to the biblical narrative because it establishes the basis for relationship, covenant, and partnership with God.

Romans 12:2—"Do not conform to the pattern of this world, but be transformed by the renewing of your mind. Then you will be able to test and approve what God's will is—His good, pleasing, and perfect will."

This verse speaks directly to alignment. It challenges us to break away from worldly patterns and be transformed by renewing our minds so that we can discern and walk in God's will. Alignment involves a radical shift in thinking, a reorientation of our priorities, and a redefinition of our values based on God's Word.

Examples of Alignment in the Bible

Throughout Scripture, we see numerous examples of alignment with God. These stories provide insight into what alignment looks like and the blessings that flow from walking in harmony with God's will:

- **Abraham's Alignment in Faith**: Abraham is often called the "father of faith," and his life demonstrates what it means to align with God's will through faith and obedience. When God called Abraham to leave his country and go to a land He would show him, Abraham aligned himself with God's command, even though he did not know where he was going (Genesis 12:1-4). His willingness to align with God's plan resulted in the establishment of a covenant that shaped the course of history.
- **Moses and the Israelites**: Moses aligned with God when he accepted the call to lead Israel out of Egypt. The entire journey from Egypt to the Promised Land was a lesson in alignment. Whenever the Israelites aligned themselves with God's instructions, they experienced His provision, protection, and presence. But when they fell out of alignment, they faced consequences and delays (Exodus 3:1-15; Numbers 14).
- **David's Heart of Alignment**: David is described as "a man after God's own heart" (1 Samuel 13:14). Despite his flaws and failures, David's life was marked by a deep desire to align with God's will. His psalms reflect his passion for God's Word, his longing for God's presence, and his commitment to walking in obedience. David's alignment with God's heart allowed him to establish a kingdom that reflected God's glory and purposes.
- **Jesus, the Perfect Example of Alignment**: Jesus is the ultimate example of alignment with God. His entire earthly ministry was

characterized by perfect obedience and alignment with the Father's will. Jesus said, "I can do nothing by myself; I can only do what I see my Father doing" (John 5:19). Even in the Garden of Gethsemane, facing the cross, Jesus aligned His will with the Father's, saying, "Not my will, but yours be done" (Luke 22:42). Jesus' life teaches us that accurate alignment with God involves surrender, sacrifice, and submission to His purposes.

The Role of the Holy Spirit in Alignment with God

Alignment with God is not something we achieve by our own efforts; it is a work of the Holy Spirit in our lives. The Holy Spirit is the one who guides us into all truth, convicts us of sin, and empowers us to live according to God's will. He is our helper, our comforter, and our guide, continually drawing us closer to the Father's heart.

John 16:13—"But when he, the Spirit of truth, comes, he will guide you into all the truth. He will not speak on his own; he will speak only what he hears, and he will tell you what is yet to come."

The Holy Spirit is essential for maintaining alignment with God. He helps us to understand God's Word, reveals God's will to us, and gives us the power to obey. Without the Holy Spirit, we would be prone to drift away from God's purposes and fall into worldly patterns. The Spirit enables us to stay on course, keeping us aligned with God's heart and direction.

How Alignment with God Affects Our Relationship with Him

When we align ourselves with God, our relationship with Him deepens. Alignment is foundational to intimacy with God because it brings us into harmony with His will, His heart, and His desires. When we align with God, we are able to experience His presence more fully, hear His voice more clearly, and see His hand at work more powerfully in our lives.

1. **Alignment Brings Clarity and Direction**

When we align with God, we gain clarity and direction. God's will is not a mystery to be solved but a path to be walked. Alignment involves surrendering our plans and desires to Him and trusting that He knows what is best for us. As we align with God, He directs our steps and leads us in paths of righteousness.

Proverbs 3:5-6—"Trust in the Lord with all your heart and lean not on your own understanding; in all your ways submit to him, and he will make your paths straight."

Clarity comes when we stop striving to figure things out on our own and start leaning on God's wisdom. Alignment with God brings a sense of peace and assurance, knowing that He is guiding us every step of the way.

2. **Alignment Opens the Door to God's Favor and Blessing**

Throughout Scripture, we see that when people align with God, they experience His favor and blessing. This is not about earning God's love; it is about positioning ourselves to receive what He desires to give. When we are aligned with God, we walk under His open heaven, where His resources, guidance, and protection flow freely.

Psalm 1:1-3—"Blessed is the one who does not walk in step with the wicked or stand in the way that sinners take or sit in the company of mockers, but whose delight is in the law of the Lord, and who meditates on his law day and night. That person is like a tree planted by streams of water, which yields its fruit in season and whose leaf does not wither—whatever they do prospers."

God's favor and blessing are by-products of alignment. When we align ourselves with His Word and His will, we are like trees planted by streams of water, constantly nourished and bearing fruit.

3. **Alignment Cultivates Intimacy and Friendship with God**

Alignment with God fosters intimacy and friendship. When we are in alignment, we are able to experience the depth of His love and the sweetness of His presence. We become more sensitive to His voice, more aware of His leading, and more attuned to His heart.

John 15:14-15—"You are my friends if you do what I command. I no longer call you servants because a servant does not know his master's business. Instead, I have called you friends, for everything that I learned from my Father I have made known to you."

Jesus calls us friends, not servants when we align ourselves with His commandments. This friendship is marked by mutual trust, shared purpose, and deep intimacy. Alignment with God leads us to a place where we are not just doing His work but are participating in His life.

4. **Alignment Empowers Us to Fulfill Our Calling**

Each of us has a unique calling and purpose from God, but we can only fulfill that calling when we are aligned with Him. When we walk in alignment with God, we are positioned to operate in the gifts and anointing He has given us. Alignment ensures that we are in the right place, at the right time, doing the right thing according to His will.

Ephesians 2:10—"For we are God's handiwork, created in Christ Jesus to do good works, which God prepared in advance for us to do."

God has prepared good works for us to walk in, but those works require us to be in alignment with Him. It is through alignment that we discover our unique calling and step into the fullness of what God has prepared for us.

Practical Steps for Aligning with God

Alignment with God is not automatic; it requires intentionality, discipline, and a desire to pursue Him. Here are some practical steps to help align ourselves with God:

1. Seek God's Face Daily

Alignment with God begins with seeking Him daily. This means setting aside time to pray, read His Word, and listen to His voice. The more we seek God, the more we come to understand His heart and His will for our lives.

Matthew 6:33—"But seek first his kingdom and his righteousness, and all these things will be given to you as well."

Seeking God's face is about prioritizing Him above all else. It is about making Him the center of our lives and allowing everything else to flow from that place of intimacy with Him.

2. Meditate on God's Word

God's Word is the primary way He reveals His will to us. When we meditate on His Word, we align our thoughts with His thoughts and our desires with His desires. The Word of God is a lamp to our feet and a light to our path (Psalm 119:105). It guides us, corrects us, and aligns us with His truth.

Joshua 1:8—"Keep this Book of the Law always on your lips; meditate on it day and night, so that you may be careful to do everything written in it. Then you will be prosperous and successful."

Meditation on God's Word involves more than reading it; it consists of allowing it to penetrate our hearts, transform our minds, and shape our actions.

3. **Listen to the Holy Spirit**

The Holy Spirit is our guide, and we must learn to listen to His promptings and guidance. Alignment with God involves being sensitive to the Holy Spirit's voice and being quick to obey His leadership. This requires cultivating a relationship with the Holy Spirit, being aware of His presence, and following His direction.

Isaiah 30:21—"Whether you turn to the right or to the left, your ears will hear a voice behind you, saying, 'This is the way; walk in it.'»

The Holy Spirit will guide us if we are willing to listen. He will direct us in the paths we should take and align us with God's purposes.

4. **Surrender Your Will**

Alignment with God requires surrendering our own will and desires. It is about saying, "Not my will, but Yours be done" (Luke 22:42). Surrender is not always easy, but it is necessary for alignment. It involves trusting God's wisdom and submitting to His authority, even when it challenges our understanding or comfort.

Proverbs 16:3—"Commit to the Lord whatever you do, and he will establish your plans."

Surrender means letting go of control and allowing God to direct our steps. It is trusting that His plans are better than ours and that He knows what is best for us.

5. **Stay in the Community**

Alignment with God is not meant to be done in isolation. God created us for the community, and He often speaks to us and aligns us through the counsel and encouragement of other believers. Being in a community of faith helps us stay accountable, encourages us in our walk, and provides wisdom and guidance.

Hebrews 10:24-25—"And let us consider how we may spur one another on toward love and good deeds, not giving up meeting together, as some are in the habit of doing, but encouraging one another—and all the more as you see the Day approaching."

The community provides support, correction, and encouragement as we pursue alignment with God. It reminds us that we are not alone on this journey.

The Transformational Impact of Alignment with God

Alignment with God is transformative. When we align ourselves with Him, we experience a deep and profound change in every area of our lives.

1. **Transformation of Character**

Alignment with God transforms our character to reflect His. As we align with God, the fruit of the Spirit—love, joy, peace, patience, kindness, goodness, faithfulness, gentleness, and self-control—becomes more evident in our lives (Galatians 5:22-23).

2. **Transformation of Relationships**

Alignment with God transforms our relationships. When we are aligned with God's heart, we are better equipped to love, serve, and forgive others. Our relationships are marked by grace, compassion, and humility, reflecting the character of Christ.

3. **Transformation of Purpose**

Alignment with God gives us a clear sense of purpose. We are no longer aimlessly wandering but are living with intentionality and focus. Our lives are directed by God's will, and our actions are aligned with His purposes.

4. **Transformation of Impact**

When we align with God, our impact on the world around us is magnified. Our prayers become more effective, our witness becomes more powerful, and our lives become a testimony to God's goodness and glory. We become vessels through which God's Kingdom is manifested on earth.

The Call to Align with God

Alignment with God is a daily journey of surrender, obedience, and intimacy. It is a call to walk in step with the Holy Spirit, to seek His face, and to live according to His Word. As we align ourselves with God, we experience His presence, His power, and His purpose in ways that transform us and those around us.

May we respond to this call with humility and faith, continually seeking to align our hearts, minds, and actions with the will of God. In this alignment, we find true peace, true purpose, and true partnership with the Creator of the universe.

CHAPTER 5

The Handshake and the House of God

In the journey of faith, understanding the profound relationship between the Divine Handshake and the House of God is crucial. The House of God is not just a physical location; it is both a personal and corporate experience of God's presence, purpose, and power. This chapter explores the biblical foundation of the House of God, its significance as a gateway between heaven and earth, and how it relates to the Divine Handshake—our partnership and covenant with God.

The House of God: The Meeting Place of Heaven and Earth
The concept of the House of God is first introduced in **Genesis 28**, when Jacob dreams of a stairway resting on the earth, reaching heaven, with angels ascending and descending on it. Above it stands the Lord, who speaks promises over Jacob's life and descendants.

Genesis 28:16-17—"When Jacob awoke from his sleep, he thought, 'Surely the Lord is in this place, and I was not aware of it.' He was afraid and said, 'How awesome is this place! This is none other than the house of God; this is the gate of heaven.'"

Jacob's encounter provides us with the first glimpse of the House of God as a sacred meeting place between heaven and earth. It is here that the natural and the supernatural intersect, where God's presence is manifest, and His promises are spoken. Jacob realizes that this "house" is not merely a physical structure but a divine portal, a gateway for angelic activity and divine communication. It represents a **transition point between two realms**—the earthly and the heavenly.

The House of God: A Revelation of God's Presence

Jacob's reaction reveals a fundamental truth about the House of God—it requires a revelation to understand. Many can be in the midst of God's presence and still be unaware of it. Just as Jacob said, "Surely the Lord is in this place, and I was not aware of it," so too can we miss the divine if we lack revelation.

Without revelation, even in the House of God, we can remain blind to the activity of heaven around us. This is why churches can have people sitting next to each other with vastly different experiences—one might be receiving a fresh revelation of God, while the other is lost in distraction.

The Function of the House of God: Operating at the Edge of Two Worlds

The House of God is designed to operate on the edge of two worlds: heaven and earth. It is more than a mere gathering place; it is a **gate, a transition point** where the divine intersects with the human. In this sacred space, angelic beings ascend and descend, carrying out God's will and fulfilling His purposes.

In Jacob's vision, he saw angels ascending and descending on what is often referred to as "Jacob's ladder." This is a prophetic picture of what the House of God is meant to be—a place of **heavenly activity** where God's will is being accomplished on earth as it is in heaven. When we understand the significance of the House of God, we see it as more than a location but as a spiritual reality that carries the weight of God's authority and purpose.

Jesus: The Fulfillment of the House of God

Centuries after Jacob's dream, Jesus Himself embodies the ultimate fulfillment of the House of God. In the Gospel of John, Jesus refers to Himself as the new temple, the dwelling place of God among men.

John 1:14—"The Word became flesh and made His dwelling among us. We have seen His glory, the glory of the one and only Son, who came from the Father, full of grace and truth."

The word "dwelling" here is significant. It means "to tabernacle" or "to pitch a tent." Jesus became the living, breathing House of God, carrying the entire presence, power, and authority of heaven wherever He went. He was the embodiment of the intersection of heaven and earth. In Him, the fullness of God dwelled bodily.

John 1:51—"He then added, 'Very truly I tell you, you will see heaven open, and the angels of God ascending and descending on the Son of Man.'"

Jesus is referencing Jacob's vision, revealing Himself as the reality of what Jacob saw in his dream. Jesus is the bridge, the ladder, the way in which heaven and earth meet. In His life, death, and resurrection, Jesus demonstrated what it meant to live in constant alignment with the Father's will, continuously bringing heaven to earth.

The Ongoing Fulfillment: The Church as the House of God

While Jesus was the initial fulfillment of the House of God, He was not the ultimate fulfillment. The Church—His body, His followers—became the continuing fulfillment of this divine reality. When we are born again, and the Holy Spirit dwells within us, we become the House of God. Each believer is a living stone, and collectively, we form a spiritual house.

1 Corinthians 3:16—«Don't you know that you yourselves are God's temple and that God's Spirit dwells in your midst?"

The revelation of being the House of God is both **personal and corporate**. Individually, we are temples of the Holy Spirit, and collectively, we are being built together to become a holy dwelling for God's presence. The Church is not a building or a denomination; it is the living, breathing Body of Christ on earth, meant to carry His presence and advance His Kingdom.

The Tension of the Personal and the Corporate

There exists a tension between the personal and the corporate aspects of the House of God. On one end of the spectrum, some believe that their relationship with God is solely personal and does not require participation in the community of faith. On the other end, others are so entrenched in the institutional church that they lose sight of their personal relationship with God.

The **Divine Handshake** bridges this tension. It is a covenant that binds the personal and the corporate together. We cannot fully be the House of God on our own; we need each other. We are not meant to function in isolation; we are called to be a body, interconnected and interdependent. Just as Jesus is the head, and we are the body, we need one another to fulfill God's purposes.

Zeal for the House of God: Jesus' Cleansing of the Temple

The importance of the House of God is underscored by Jesus' actions when He cleansed the temple. Twice in His ministry, Jesus entered the temple and drove out those who were desecrating it with their commercial activities. His actions were not just about cleansing a physical building; they were a prophetic declaration about the nature of His Father's house.

John 2:16-17—"To those who sold doves he said, 'Get these out of here! Stop turning my Father's house into a market!' His disciples remembered that it is written: 'Zeal for your house will consume me.'"

Jesus' zeal for the House of God was not just about the temple in Jerusalem. It was about the purity, holiness, and purpose of God's dwelling place—whether in a building or in His people. His righteous anger against the misuse of the temple was a foreshadowing of the holiness He desires in us as His living temples.

The House of God: A Place of Transformation and Encounter

The House of God is more than a place; it is an experience, a state of being. It is where heaven touches earth, where God's presence transforms lives, where His Word is declared, and where His power is demonstrated. The House of God is where we encounter the living God, where our lives are transformed by His presence, and where we are equipped to go out and be His witnesses in the world.

To be the House of God means to live in alignment with His will, to carry His presence, and to be agents of His Kingdom. It means being a place where angelic activity is expected, where miracles, signs, and wonders are expected, and where lives are continually being transformed.

The Divine Handshake and the House of God

The Divine Handshake represents our **covenant partnership** with God. It is the agreement between heaven and earth to work together to accomplish God's will. The House of God is the arena where this partnership is realized. It is where we, as God's people, take His hand and co-labor with Him to see His Kingdom come and His will be done on earth as it is in heaven.

To fully grasp the Divine Handshake, we must understand that it involves both the personal and corporate dimensions of faith. It requires us to embrace our personal relationship with God and engage in the community of believers. It's about **being the House of God**—individually and together.

1. The House of God as a Place of Surrender
The House of God is a place where we surrender our wills and align with God's purposes. It is where we lay down our agendas and take up His. In the Divine Handshake, we submit to His authority and allow Him to shape us into His image.

2. The House of God as a Place of Worship and Intercession
The House of God is a place of worship and intercession, where we offer spiritual sacrifices and stand in the gap for others. It is a place where we call down heaven to earth, where we declare His promises and push back the darkness.

3. The House of God as a Place of Empowerment and Sending
The House of God is also a place of empowerment and sending. It is where believers are equipped, trained, and released into their destinies. It is a launching pad for Kingdom advancement. In the Divine Handshake, we are not just recipients of God's grace; we are participants in His mission.

Embracing the Divine Handshake in the House of God
The House of God is central to our understanding of the Divine Handshake. It is where heaven meets earth, where God dwells among His people, and where His Kingdom is made manifest. As the House of God, we have the responsibility to steward His presence, carry His glory, and co-labor with Him in bringing His will to pass.

May we embrace this revelation with awe and commitment, understanding that we are part of something much more significant than ourselves. As we engage in the Divine Handshake, let us be the House of God that brings heaven to earth, revealing His glory and advancing His Kingdom in every sphere of influence.

From House of God to Holy Ground

As we deepen our understanding of the House of God and the Divine Handshake, we see a powerful connection between Jesus and the cleansing of the temple. The House of God is not just a physical space; it is a sacred meeting place where heaven touches earth, where God's presence dwells, and where His people engage in pure, unadulterated worship. Jesus' dramatic act of cleansing the temple was not merely a moment of righteous anger but a declaration of what it means to be holy ground—a prophetic call to restore the House of God to its rightful purpose.

The temple cleansing reveals God's desire for His dwelling place to be pure, undivided, and holy. It speaks to the reality that as the House of God—both individually and corporately—we must be places where God's presence is welcomed and His purposes are fulfilled. Just as Jesus overturned the tables and drove out the merchants who had defiled the temple, so too must we examine our own lives and our collective gatherings as the Body of Christ. The cleansing symbolizes a powerful call to align ourselves with God's will, remove anything that corrupts our worship, and make room for a fresh move of His Spirit.

The impact of the temple cleansing goes beyond the physical temple in Jerusalem; it challenges us today as the living stones that make up the spiritual house of God. It is a call to reclaim our role in the Divine Handshake—co-laboring with God to establish His Kingdom on earth. As we move forward, let us consider what it means to indeed be the House of God, cleansed, consecrated, and committed to His purposes. In this, we find the true essence of what it means to bring heaven to earth, living as holy ground where God's glory dwells and His will is done.

The **temple cleansing** by Jesus is one of the most powerful and symbolic acts recorded in the Gospels. It was not only a moment of righteous indignation but also a profound declaration of Jesus' authority, His zeal for God's holiness, and a prophetic act that signaled a significant shift in how people would understand worship, sacrifice, and the very presence of God. The impact of this event is both immediate and far-reaching, affecting the socio-religious context of the time, the theological understanding of God's dwelling place, and the spiritual lives of believers.

The Immediate Impact: A Confrontation with Corruption

At its core, the **temple cleansing** was a confrontation against the corruption and commercialization that had infiltrated the sacred space meant for worship. In both instances recorded in the Gospels (John 2:13-22, Matthew 21:12-17), Jesus entered the temple courts and saw merchants selling animals for sacrifice and money changers conducting business, turning the house of God into a marketplace. This was not just about people buying and selling; it was about exploiting worshippers, particularly the poor, who had come to offer sacrifices to God.

Jesus' response was one of **righteous anger**. He overturned tables, drove out the money changers, and rebuked those who were desecrating the temple, saying, "It is written, 'My house will be called a house of prayer,' but you are making it a den of robbers" (Matthew 21:13).

1. Purification of Worship

The immediate impact of Jesus' actions was a dramatic **purification of worship**. He was restoring the sacredness of the temple, reclaiming it as a house of prayer rather than a den of thieves. This act would have struck at the heart of the religious leaders, exposing their hypocrisy and greed. By cleansing the temple, Jesus was calling Israel back to pure worship, free from exploitation and corruption.

2. Challenge to Religious Authority

The temple cleansing also directly challenged the religious authorities of the time. The priests, scribes, and Pharisees had allowed the commercial activities to take place, likely receiving a share of the profits. Jesus' actions undermined their authority, exposing their failure to maintain the holiness of God's house. This act of defiance against the religious establishment set the stage for the growing tension between Jesus and the Jewish leaders, eventually leading to His arrest and crucifixion.

3. Declaration of Messianic Authority

By cleansing the temple, Jesus was making a bold declaration of His **messianic authority**. The temple was the center of Jewish religious life, and only someone with authority more significant than the temple could do what Jesus did. In doing so, He was asserting His divine right to purify the temple and redefine its purpose. This act was a sign of His authority as the Son of God, foreshadowing His ultimate mission to cleanse humanity of sin.

The Theological Impact: Redefining the Dwelling Place of God

The **temple cleansing** was not just about clearing out the merchants; it was a prophetic act that redefined the concept of the **dwelling place of God**. For centuries, the temple in Jerusalem had been the physical and symbolic center of Jewish worship, where sacrifices were offered, and God's presence was believed to dwell in the Holy of Holies. Jesus' actions, however, pointed to a new reality.

1. From Physical Temple to Spiritual Temple

When Jesus said, "Destroy this temple, and I will raise it again in three days," (John 2:19), He was speaking of His body, not the physical structure. This statement was misunderstood by His listeners, who thought He meant the physical temple building. Jesus was, in fact, prophesying about His death and resurrection, indicating that He Himself would become the new temple—the new dwelling place of God on earth.

This shift meant that the physical temple in Jerusalem would no longer be the focal point of God's presence. Instead, Jesus, through His death and resurrection, would establish a new covenant where **God's Spirit would dwell in the hearts of believers**. The cleansing of the temple was a prophetic act foreshadowing this spiritual reality.

2. The End of the Sacrificial System
By cleansing the temple, Jesus also signaled the end of the Old Covenant sacrificial system. The buying and selling of sacrificial animals were at the core of the temple's economic activity, but Jesus' actions indicated that a new sacrifice was about to take place—His own death on the cross. His sacrifice would be once and for all, eliminating the need for continual animal sacrifices. This was a **radical redefinition** of how humanity would approach God—no longer through the blood of bulls and goats but through the blood of Christ.

3. A Call to Holiness and Pure Worship
The temple cleansing was also a call to holiness and pure worship. Jesus was restoring the temple to its original purpose—a place of prayer, worship, and communion with God. This was a stark reminder that God is holy and that His presence cannot coexist with corruption, greed, or exploitation. It is a call to believers throughout the ages to ensure that their lives, as the new temples of God, remain pure, holy, and set apart for His purposes.

The Spiritual Impact: The House of God and the Divine Handshake
The cleansing of the temple has a profound spiritual impact on understanding our role as the **House of God** and our participation in the **Divine Handshake**—the covenant relationship between God and His people.

1. The Temple as a Symbol of Our Lives
As the New Testament reveals, our bodies are now the temples of the Holy Spirit (1 Corinthians 6:19-20). Just as Jesus cleansed the physical temple,

so too does He desire to cleanse and purify our hearts and lives. The Divine Handshake involves our cooperation with God in allowing Him to cleanse us of sin, purify our motives, and align our desires with His.

The cleansing of the temple serves as a potent reminder that **God's presence requires holiness**. We are called to be set apart, living lives that reflect His glory and honor His name. This requires a continual process of self-examination, repentance, and surrender to the Holy Spirit's refining work.

2. Establishing a New Order of Worship

The cleansing of the temple also points to a new order of worship that is not tied to a specific location or ritual but is based on spirit and truth. Jesus told the Samaritan woman, "A time is coming and has now come when the true worshipers will worship the Father in spirit and truth, for they are the kind of worshipers the Father seeks" (John 4:23).

This new order of worship emphasizes **relationship over ritual** and **presence over place**. The Divine Handshake is about entering into a relationship with God where our worship is authentic, heartfelt, and guided by the Holy Spirit. It is not about external performances but about internal transformation and intimacy with God.

3. The Call to Be a House of Prayer

When Jesus cleansed the temple, He declared, "My house will be called a house of prayer for all nations" (Mark 11:17). This declaration has profound implications for us today. As the House of God, we are called to be a **people of prayer**, interceding for our communities, nations, and the world. The Divine Handshake involves partnering with God in prayer to see His Kingdom come, and He will be done on earth as it is in heaven.

The cleansing of the temple challenges us to examine our own lives and our churches. Are we places where prayer is central? Are we prioritizing communion with God and seeking His face above all else? The impact of Jesus' actions in the temple reminds us that prayer is not an optional activity; it is the lifeblood of a thriving, Spirit-filled community.

The Prophetic Impact: Preparing for a New Covenant Community

Jesus' cleansing of the temple was not only an act of purification but also a **prophetic declaration** of the new covenant community that He was establishing. This community would be marked not by a building but by the presence of God dwelling within His people. It would be a community where every believer is a priest, every home a temple, and every gathering a place where heaven meets earth.

1. A Community of Believers as Living Stones

Under the new covenant, believers are described as **living stones** being built into a spiritual house (1 Peter 2:5). The impact of the temple cleansing is that it shifts the focus from a physical structure to a spiritual community. The Divine Handshake involves believers coming together in unity, each contributing their gifts and callings to build up the Body of Christ.

2. An Invitation to Co-Labor with God

The temple cleansing was a clarion call to a deeper level of partnership with God. It was an invitation to enter into the Divine Handshake and co-labor with Him in establishing His Kingdom on earth. This involves a commitment to holiness, a dedication to prayer, and a willingness to be transformed into His likeness.

3. A Foretaste of the Coming Kingdom

Finally, the temple cleansing is a **foretaste of the coming Kingdom**, where God will dwell fully with His people. It is a prophetic picture of the ultimate cleansing that will take place when Jesus returns and establishes His eternal Kingdom. Until then, we are called to live as Kingdom citizens, bringing heaven to earth through our lives, our prayers, and our worship.

The Lasting Impact of the Temple Cleansing

The impact of Jesus' cleansing of the temple extends far beyond that singular event. It is a profound statement of God's desire for pure worship, a holy dwelling place, and a people who are entirely devoted to Him. It challenges us to examine our lives, our churches, and our communities to ensure that we are living as the actual House of God—a house of prayer, a house of purity, and a home of power.

The Divine Handshake invites us into this reality. May we respond with humility, zeal, and a renewed commitment to be the dwelling place of the Most High, reflecting His glory and advancing His Kingdom on earth.

Zeal for the House of God: The Flame that Fuels the Divine Handshake

Zeal is a fervent and intense passion for something deeply cherished. In the context of the **House of God** and the **Divine Handshake**, zeal represents an uncompromising commitment to preserving the sanctity and purpose of God's dwelling place, both within us and among us. Zeal is the fuel that drives our partnership with God—our Divine Handshake—ensuring that His Kingdom is manifested on earth as it is in heaven. It is this holy fervor that compels us to guard the purity of God's presence in our lives and our communities, aligning ourselves with His divine purpose.

Zeal as the Guardian of Holiness in the House of God

The **House of God** is meant to be a place of worship, prayer, and divine encounter. It is where heaven meets earth and where God's will is enacted. Zeal, in this context, is the protective flame that ensures the House of God remains holy, undefiled, and focused on God's purposes. When

Jesus cleansed the temple, He did so with **zeal** for His Father's house, declaring, "My house will be called a house of prayer for all nations, but you have made it a den of robbers" (**Mark 11:17**). This zeal was not a momentary burst of anger but a profound, consuming passion for the sanctity of God's dwelling place.

The act of cleansing the temple was an expression of Jesus' commitment to the House of God being a true sanctuary, a sacred space where God's presence could dwell without hindrance or corruption. This zeal is a critical component of the Divine Handshake—our covenant relationship with God—because it represents our dedication to maintaining the purity and integrity of God's presence among us.

Zeal as the Catalyst for the Divine Handshake

The **Divine Handshake** is our partnership with God, where heaven and earth align to accomplish His purposes. This partnership is not passive; it requires an active, burning zeal that propels us into action. Zeal is what drives believers to take hold of God's hand with fervency and conviction, co-laboring with Him to bring His Kingdom to earth. Without zeal, our relationship with God becomes lukewarm, our worship becomes routine, and our commitment to His purposes wanes.

Zeal ignites the fire of the Divine Handshake, ensuring that our co-laboring with God is vibrant, passionate, and fully engaged. It is zeal that moves us beyond complacency and apathy, pushing us to pursue God's heart and His will with intensity. When we are zealous for the House of God, we are not content with mere ritual or religion; we seek to create an environment—both in our personal lives and in our corporate gatherings—where God's presence is tangible, and His power is evident.

Zeal as a Unifying Force in the Body of Christ

The House of God is not just an individual reality but a collective experience. We are **living stones** being built together into a spiritual house (**1 Peter 2:5**). Zeal plays a crucial role in unifying the Body of Christ because it fosters a shared commitment to God's purposes. When believers are zealous for the House of God, they are driven by a common desire to see God glorified, His presence magnified, and His will accomplished.

Zeal creates a culture of **passionate worship**, fervent prayer, and radical obedience. It inspires believers to lay down personal agendas and preferences in favor of God's divine plan. This shared zeal binds us together, strengthening our partnership with one another and with God. In this way, zeal is both a personal and corporate force that sustains the Divine Handshake and keeps us aligned with God's heart.

Zeal and the Call to Action

Zeal for the House of God is not just an internal emotion; it is a call to action. It compels us to actively engage in the work of the Kingdom, to stand against anything that defiles or distracts from God's purposes, and to build up His Church as a holy, vibrant, and dynamic community. This zeal demands a response—it challenges us to cleanse our own "temples," repent of complacency, and commit fully to the mission of God.

In the **Divine Handshake**, zeal is the passion that drives us to be fully engaged in our covenant with God. It is what compels us to fight for the purity of God's House, to protect the sacredness of His presence, and to partner with Him in bringing His will to pass. As we cultivate zeal, we become more aligned with God's heart, more effective in His purposes, and more prepared to be His hands and feet on earth.

The Power of Zeal in the House of God

Zeal for the House of God is the flame that keeps the Divine Handshake alive. It is a fervent, holy passion that refuses to settle for anything less than God's best. This zeal is not about self-righteous anger; it is about a deep love for God's presence, His people, and His purposes. It is about co-laboring with God to build a spiritual house where His glory dwells, where His name is honored, and where His Kingdom is advanced. May we, as God's people, be consumed with zeal for His House and fully engaged in the Divine Handshake, bringing heaven to earth through our lives and our communities.

Impact of Corporate Zeal: A Unified Force for God's Kingdom

Corporate zeal refers to the collective passion, fervor, and commitment of a community of believers who are united in their pursuit of God's purposes. When zeal moves beyond the individual and becomes a shared experience within the Body of Christ, it creates a powerful force that can transform not only the Church but also the world around it. The impact of corporate zeal is profound, as it ignites revival, fosters unity, propels mission, and establishes God's Kingdom on earth in ways that individual zeal alone cannot achieve.

1. Igniting Revival and Spiritual Awakening

Corporate zeal has the power to ignite **revival** and **spiritual awakening** within a church, a city, or even a nation. When a community of believers is united in passionate pursuit of God's presence, a supernatural atmosphere is created where the Holy Spirit moves freely. This zeal becomes contagious, spreading from person to person, stirring hearts, and awakening a collective hunger for more of God. Revival is not just an emotional experience; it is the tangible result of a people who are burning with a shared desire to see God's glory manifested in their midst.

In the Book of Acts, we see how the corporate zeal of the early Church led to an outpouring of the Holy Spirit on the Day of Pentecost. The disciples were gathered together "with one accord" (**Acts 2:1**), waiting and praying fervently for the promised Holy Spirit. Their unified zeal created an environment for the Holy Spirit to descend, filling them with power and boldness, which resulted in the conversion of thousands and the birth of the early Church. This same corporate zeal can ignite revival today, bringing about supernatural encounters, miracles, and mass salvations.

2. Fostering Unity and Strengthening the Body of Christ

Corporate zeal fosters **unity** within the Body of Christ. When believers are collectively zealous for the House of God, they are driven by a common purpose—to glorify God, advance His Kingdom, and see His will done on earth. This shared zeal diminishes personal agendas and promotes a culture of selflessness, where each member is more concerned with the needs of others and the greater mission of the Church.

Ephesians 4:3 exhorts believers to "make every effort to keep the unity of the Spirit through the bond of peace." Corporate zeal aligns believers with the heart of God and each other, creating a bond that transcends individual differences and preferences. It builds a strong, resilient Church that can withstand external pressures, internal conflicts, and spiritual warfare. A unified Church is a powerful Church, and corporate zeal is the driving force that binds the Church together, making it practical and impactful.

3. Propelling Mission and Evangelistic Outreach

Corporate zeal also **propels mission** and **evangelistic outreach**. A church filled with zeal is not content to stay within the four walls of a building; it is driven to take the Gospel to the ends of the earth. When zeal becomes a shared experience, it mobilizes the entire congregation to be actively engaged in the Great Commission—making disciples of all nations, baptizing them, and teaching them to obey everything Christ commanded (**Matthew 28:19-20**).

This collective zeal equips and empowers believers to step out in boldness, share their faith, serve their communities, and engage in acts of compassion and justice. It compels the Church to look beyond itself and see the world through the eyes of Christ, who came to seek and save the lost. Corporate zeal transforms a passive church into an active, dynamic force that advances God's Kingdom in tangible and transformative ways.

4. Establishing God's Kingdom on Earth

Corporate zeal plays a crucial role in establishing **God's Kingdom** on earth. When a community of believers is zealous for God's presence, power, and purposes, it creates a spiritual atmosphere where God's Kingdom can be manifested. This zeal aligns the Church with God's will, allowing His authority to flow through His people to bring about healing, deliverance, transformation, and justice.

In this context, corporate zeal is not just about emotional excitement; it is about **kingdom alignment**. It ensures that the Church is fully surrendered to God's will and fully engaged in His mission. The result is a powerful demonstration of God's Kingdom on earth as it is in heaven. This could be seen in the early Church, where their corporate zeal resulted in a community marked by radical generosity, signs, wonders, and a deep sense of awe and reverence for God (**Acts 2:42-47**).

5. Cultivating a Culture of Prayer and Intercession

Corporate zeal creates a **culture of prayer and intercession** within the Church. A zealous congregation understands that prayer is the engine that drives everything. When believers are united in fervent prayer, they align themselves with God's heart and become partners in His purposes. This kind of prayer is not just about petitioning God for needs but about standing in the gap for others, interceding for nations, and declaring God's promises over situations.

A Church that is zealous in prayer becomes a **spiritual powerhouse**, capable of shifting atmospheres, breaking strongholds, and ushering in God's will on earth. It becomes a place where spiritual breakthroughs happen regularly, where the impossible becomes possible, and where God's presence is tangibly felt. This corporate zeal for prayer and intercession is critical in sustaining revival, advancing the mission, and establishing God's Kingdom.

6. Inspiring Sacrificial Service and Generosity

When a community is filled with corporate zeal, it inspires **sacrificial service** and **generosity**. Believers are willing to lay down their time, resources, and even their lives for the sake of the Gospel. They understand that the mission of God requires everyone's participation and that true zeal is demonstrated in action, not just words. This was evident in the early Church, where believers sold their possessions and gave to anyone in need, ensuring that "there were no needy persons among them" (**Acts 4:34**).

Corporate zeal shifts the focus from self to others, from getting to giving, and from comfort to sacrifice. It produces a community that is marked by love, selflessness, and radical generosity. This kind of zeal not only meets the needs within the Church but also becomes a powerful witness to the world of the transforming power of the Gospel.

7. Breaking Down Strongholds and Advancing Spiritual Warfare

Corporate zeal is a formidable weapon in **spiritual warfare**. When a church is zealous for God and His purposes, it stands united against the forces of darkness. This zeal becomes a collective force that breaks down spiritual strongholds, pushes back the kingdom of darkness, and establishes the rule and reign of Christ in every sphere of life.

Corporate zeal fuels the faith needed to believe in miracles, healings, and deliverances. It creates an atmosphere where spiritual gifts are activated, and believers are emboldened to operate in their God-given authority. It turns a passive congregation into an army of warriors who are ready to contend for their cities, families, and nations, knowing that they are backed by the power of God.

The Unstoppable Force of Corporate Zeal

Corporate zeal is more than a collective feeling; it is an **unstoppable force** that God uses to build His Church, advance His Kingdom, and transform the world. It is the collective burning passion of God's people to see His glory revealed, His will accomplished, and His name exalted. When a church is united in zeal, it becomes a house of prayer, a center of revival, a beacon of light, and a force for change.

The **Divine Handshake** is magnified in the context of corporate zeal. When we join hands with God and with one another in fervent commitment to His purposes, nothing is impossible. This shared zeal propels us into deeper intimacy with God, more vital unity with each other, and greater effectiveness in the world. May we, as the Body of Christ, be filled with a zeal that consumes us, empowers us, and sends us out to bring heaven to earth.

CHAPTER 6

The Venue of the Handshake: Where Divine and Human Purpose Align

In our exploration of the Divine Handshake, we realize that this sacred exchange does not occur in a void. It takes place in a divinely designated venue where heaven touches the earth, and God's eternal purposes intersect with humanity's deepest needs. This venue is the **House of God**, a place where believers gather, grow, and are empowered to carry out God's work on earth. It is here, in this holy and vibrant space, that the Divine Handshake is made manifest through our collective worship, our shared mission, and our unwavering commitment to one another. Let us delve deeply into the essence of this venue, understanding its biblical roots, its transformative power, and how it serves as a catalyst for God's Kingdom to be established on earth.

1. **Cleansing the Temple: Reclaiming Sacred Space for Divine Purposes**
The account of Jesus cleansing the temple in **John 2:13-22** provides a vivid illustration of what it means to honor the venue of the Divine Handshake. During the Passover in Jerusalem, Jesus entered the temple and was confronted by a scene of commercialism and exploitation. Merchants were selling oxen, sheep, and doves, while money changers were doing business. Seeing this, Jesus made a whip of cords, drove them out, overturned their tables, and declared, "Take these things away; do not make my Father's house a house of trade" (**John 2:16**).

- **A Place Set Apart**: This decisive moment wasn't just an act of righteous indignation; it was a declaration that God's house must remain a sacred space reserved for worship, prayer, and divine encounter. The temple was to be a place where God's holiness was honored and His presence revered. Jesus' actions remind us that the venue of the Divine Handshake—the House of God—must be kept holy, free from distractions and worldly contamination. This is where God's people meet with Him in purity and reverence.
- **Zeal for the House of God**: "Zeal for your house will consume me," His disciples remembered, quoting **Psalm 69:9**. This zeal that burned within Jesus is the same passion that must ignite our hearts today. We must be zealous for God's house, not as a physical structure but as the spiritual hub where heaven meets earth. It should be a place where the atmosphere is charged with worship, prayer, and the glory of God. A space where miracles are birthed, lives are transformed, and communities are revived.
- **Restoring Holiness and Purpose**: The cleansing of the temple is a call for us to examine and cleanse our own "temples continually»—our lives, our homes, and our church communities. Anything that detracts from God's glory must be driven out. Are we turning the house of God into a place of personal agenda or entertainment, or is it a sanctuary of surrender and holiness?

2. Living Stones: Building a Spiritual House Together

In **1 Peter 2:5**, we read, "You also, like living stones, are being built into a spiritual house to be a holy priesthood, offering spiritual sacrifices acceptable to God through Jesus Christ." Here, Peter uses the metaphor of "living stones" to describe believers being shaped and positioned together to build a spiritual house—a vibrant, living community dedicated to God.

- **The Nature of Living Stones**: Each of us is a "living stone," uniquely crafted by the Master Builder. Our individuality and diversity are not just celebrated but essential in building God's house. A living stone finds its true purpose and identity when connected with others. Alone, a stone is just a stone, but when joined with others, it becomes part of a magnificent structure—a holy dwelling for God.
- **The Power of Connection**: The life of a living stone is validated through its connectivity. Just as a brick must be cemented together with others to form a sturdy wall, so too must we, as living stones, connect deeply with one another to build a solid spiritual house. This is why community is not just a good idea; it is essential. The venue of the Divine Handshake flourishes in unity. When we worship, pray, and serve together, we create an environment where God's presence dwells powerfully.
- **Spiritual Sacrifices in Community**: In this spiritual house, we offer "spiritual sacrifices"—our prayers, worship, service, and lives surrendered to God. This is not something we do in isolation; it is a communal act. Just as in the days of the early church, where believers "devoted themselves to the apostles' teaching and to fellowship, to the breaking of bread and to prayer" (**Acts 2:42**), we too are called to gather, share, and grow together. This shared life is the essence of the venue where the Divine Handshake takes place.

3. Ecclesia and Oikos: The Two Dimensions of the Church

To fully understand the venue of the handshake, we must grasp two critical concepts in the New Testament that describe the church: **Ecclesia** and **Oikos**.

A. Ecclesia: The Global Assembly of Believers

"Ecclesia" refers to the universal, worldwide body of believers known as the "called-out ones." Jesus said in **Matthew 16:18**, "And

I tell you that you are Peter, and on this rock, I will build my church, and the gates of Hades will not overcome it."

- **A Gathering with Divine Purpose**: The term Ecclesia was initially used to describe an assembly of citizens called out from their homes to a public place for the purpose of deliberation. This gives us a picture of a church gathered with a purpose—to discuss, decide, and impact society in a transformative way. When we gather as Ecclesia, we are more than a congregation; we are a council for heaven's agenda on earth.
- **United Against Darkness**: The promise that the "gates of Hades will not overcome it" speaks to the collective strength and authority of the Ecclesia. Our gatherings are not just for spiritual nourishment but are strategic gatherings where we align with God's purposes to push back the darkness and bring heaven's light into our world. This is why our unity and shared purpose are vital; we are an army positioned to take spiritual ground.

B. Oikos: The Local Expression of God's Household

"Oikos" refers to the local expression of the church—the household of faith. It represents a community of believers who share a common spiritual kinship and a joint mission.

- **A Family of Faith**: The Oikos is more than a congregation; it is a family. **1 Peter 2:5** describes believers as being built into a "spiritual house." The members of this house are like family, connected through spiritual kinship, shared experiences, and a common purpose. This family unit is where spiritual growth happens, where disciples are made, and where believers are equipped to live out their divine calling.
- **Encouraging One Another to Good Works**: **Hebrews 10:24-25** reminds us of the importance of meeting together to encourage one another toward love and good deeds.

The Oikos is where we spur each other on, challenge one another to grow, and celebrate each other's victories. This mutual encouragement and accountability are crucial for spiritual maturity and are at the heart of the venue of the Divine Handshake.

4. **The Role of Community: The Heartbeat of the Venue**

The House of God—the venue for the Divine Handshake—finds its strength and vitality in the community. Community is the lifeblood of the church, and it is within this shared life that the Divine Handshake is most powerfully manifested.

- **A Place of Deep Connection**: Community is where people know each other beyond the surface, where relationships are deep and authentic. It is a place where we are known, where we serve one another, and where we support each other through all seasons of life. It is where our joys are doubled, and our sorrows halved.
- **Celebrating Diversity While Maintaining Unity**: The beauty of a community lies in its diversity. We are a diverse body—different backgrounds, races, and experiences—but our unity in Christ is what binds us together. If diversity is our strength, then the potential for division can be our weakness. That is why our commitment must be to the covenant of unity in Christ rather than to any style, tradition, or preference.
- **Constructive Feedback and Accountability**: In a healthy community, there is room for growth, accountability, and constructive feedback. We all have blind spots—areas of our lives that we cannot see clearly. In community, we have the opportunity to speak into each other's lives, helping each other to grow and become the people God has called us to be. As Proverbs says, "As iron sharpens iron, so one person sharpens another" (**Proverbs 27:17**).

5. **Learning from David's Mighty Men: A Model for Reformation**

The story of David's mighty men in **1 Chronicles 12** is a profound example of how God uses committed, courageous, and unified individuals to bring about reformation and revival.

- **Willing to Be Molded and Shaped**: David's mighty men were not only warriors but also men of revelation. They were willing to be taught, challenged, and shaped. Their willingness to submit to authority and to be reshaped was the catalyst for Israel's reformation. In the same way, we must be willing to be molded and shaped within the venue of the House of God.
- **Reformation Begins with Us**: The venue of the Divine Handshake—the House of God—is where reformation begins. Just as David's men were catalysts for change in their generation, we too are called to be catalysts for reformation in our time. But this requires a willingness to be spurred on toward good deeds, to grow in faith, and to take risks for God's Kingdom.

6. **The House of God: The Ultimate Venue of Divine Encounter**

The House of God is the ultimate venue of divine encounter and transformation. It is the palace of submission, the place of authority, the ground of surrender, the sanctuary of holiness, and the place where friendship with God flourishes. It is the venue where we come to know, without a shadow of a doubt, that we are God's beloved.

- **A Place of Submission and Authority**: In the House of God, we learn to submit to God's will and to recognize His authority over our lives. It is a place where we lay down our agendas and align ourselves with God's divine purposes.
- **A Place of Holiness and Friendship**: Holiness is not just about moral purity; it is about being set apart for God's purposes. In the House of God, we cultivate this holiness as we draw near to Him and as we draw near to one another. It is also a place where friendship with God is deepened. Jesus no longer calls

us servants but friends because we know His heart and His plans (**John 15:15**).
- **A Place of Partnership and Right Standing**: The venue of the Divine Handshake is where we realize that we are not just workers in God's vineyard but partners with Him in His mission. It is a place where we stand in the right relationship with God, fully aware of our identity as His children and His ambassadors.

Building the Venue for the Divine Handshake Together

As we consider the venue of the Divine Handshake—the House of God—we must ask ourselves, are we creating an environment where God's presence is honored, His people are connected, and His purposes are fulfilled? The House of God is not just a building; it is a living, breathing community where heaven meets earth. It is a place of transformation, empowerment, and mission.

May we embrace this venue with zeal and commitment, always seeking to honor God, connect deeply with one another, and fulfill our divine calling. For it is in this sacred space that the Divine Handshake becomes a reality, where God's Kingdom is established, and His will is done on earth as it is in heaven.

CHAPTER 7

The Divine Handshake Breaks the Orphan Mindset

Romans 8:14-19

14 For those who are led by the Spirit of God are the children of God. 15 The Spirit you received does not make you slaves so that you live in fear again; instead, the Spirit you received brought about your adoption to sonship. And by him we cry, "Abba, Father." 16 The Spirit himself testifies with our spirit that we are God's children. 17 Now if we are children, then we are heirs—heirs of God and co-heirs with Christ, if indeed we share in his sufferings in order that we may also share in his glory. 18 I consider that our present sufferings are not worth comparing with the glory that will be revealed in us. 19 For the creation waits in eager expectation for the children of God to be revealed.

Since the resurrection, God has extended His hand to us, giving us the opportunity for heaven to come to earth. This divine invitation is at the heart of what we call the **Divine Handshake**. It is a powerful gesture where God reaches out, calling us into deeper relationships and co-laboring with Him. It's part of the prayer Jesus taught us to pray, which we call the Lord's Prayer but is really "our prayer":

"Our Father, who is in heaven, Hallowed be your name. Your kingdom comes, you will be done on earth as it is in heaven..."
This prayer is answered when we receive a revelation and an understanding of the Divine Handshake—when we embrace our role as co-laborers with God and step into the fullness of our identity in Him.

Toward the end of His earthly life, Jesus offered His disciples the ultimate promotion. He told them that they were no longer servants but friends. This shift in status—from servants to friends—was monumental. Jesus brought them into His inner circle, giving them access to His life, His heart, and His divine secrets. They had proven themselves worthy of this promotion, and with it came a shift in focus: from being apprentices to being commissioned to execute the will of the Father.

They were given access to the secrets in the heart of God because **revelation comes from intimacy**. Jesus made a clear distinction between the two positions—servants and friends. **Servants** do not know what their master is doing. They do not have access to the intimate, personal realm of their master. Servants are **task-oriented**; their primary focus is obedience, for their survival and success depend on it. But **friends** have a different focus. While obedience is essential for friends, the more significant concern is not about disobeying but about disappointing.

As Jesus said in **John 15:14**, *"You are my friends if you do what I command you."*

Friends move from the commandments to the presence, from the assignment to the relationship, from "what I do for Him" to "how my choices affect Him." This is the essence of the **Divine Handshake**—partnering with God in a relationship of deep intimacy and purpose.

But today, we want to talk about yet another promotion that God has for us. How can we get better than being called a friend of God? It is when we understand that we are not just friends but **sons and daughters of God**. This brings us to a profound truth: the necessity of **Breaking the Orphan Spirit**.

The Orphan Spirit: A Crisis of Identity and Belonging

The term "orphan spirit" is often misunderstood. It is not limited to those who have lost their biological parents; it is a spiritual condition that affects many people, even believers. Ever since Adam and Eve were alienated from God the Father in the Garden of Eden, an **orphan spirit** has permeated the earth, causing untold damage. By "orphan," I am referring to a sense of abandonment, loneliness, alienation, and isolation.

After the fall of Eden, the fruit of this orphan spirit was quickly evident in human history. We see it in **Cain's jealousy** and his murder of his brother Abel because God the Father did not receive his offering. This spirit of alienation has continued through the ages, and it is mainly active in contemporary society with the breakdown of the nuclear family. Large numbers of people are not only alienated from God but are also brought up without the loving care and security of their biological fathers. This has resulted in a society filled with emotional, physical, and spiritual brokenness.

Romans 8:15 tells us,

"The Spirit you received does not make you slaves so that you live in fear again; rather, the Spirit you received brought about your adoption to sonship. And by him we cry, 'Abba, Father.'"

The Manifestation of the Orphan Spirit

The **orphan spirit** manifests in various ways. Orphaned men and women often have a hard time connecting to their spouses, children, supervisors at work, and especially to those in spiritual authority. They also struggle to accept and love themselves. There are presently millions of incarcerated men and women who are living out lives of violence and rebellion because their earthly fathers abandoned them. The orphan spirit is not just a relational problem; it is a deep spiritual wound that needs healing.

The **only way** to break this orphan spirit is for people to be filled with a sense of the Father's love for them in Christ. This revelation enables them to become mature sons and daughters who serve God out of the knowledge of His undeserved grace rather than trying to earn the Father's love through performance. The orphan spirit creates a mindset of striving, competing, and trying to prove one's worth. But when we receive the Spirit of sonship, we move from trying to resting, from competing to receiving, and from earning to inheriting.

The Curse of the Orphan Spirit and the Need for Spiritual Parents

I genuinely believe that the **orphan spirit** is one of the greatest curses on the earth today. It will take the anointing of spiritual parents with great spiritual depth and authority to break and reverse this curse and initiate a generational blessing. Only when a person is healed of fatherlessness through the love of the Father can the orphan spirit be broken, allowing them to begin the process of entering into mature sonship?

Romans 8:19 states,

"For the creation waits in eager expectation for the children of God to be revealed."

Sonship is so essential that all of creation is presently crying out and groaning for the manifestation of mature sons and daughters of God. This groaning is a cosmic longing for a world restored to its original design, where God's children walk in their true identity and purpose.

The Struggle with the Orphan Spirit Among Believers

We all have an orphan spirit at some point in our lives, regardless of who raised us. We have all stewarded an orphan spirit before being adopted into the family of Christ. But even after adoption, we may continue to struggle with an orphan spirit without even realizing it. The **orphan spirit** causes one to live life as if he or she doesn't have a safe and secure place in the Father's heart. It makes a person feel they have no place of affirmation, protection, comfort, belonging, or affection.

This is why many people go from church to church or struggle to be planted in a specific community. An orphan spirit has trouble recognizing that we were created to **belong**. An orphan mindset is self-oriented, lonely, and inwardly isolated. It has no one from whom to draw a godly inheritance. It forces people to strive, achieve, compete, and earn everything they get in life. People with an orphan spirit struggle with a life of anxiety, various fears, and deep frustration.

Why We Live with an Orphan Spirit
There are many reasons why someone might live with an orphan spirit, even as a believer. Perhaps they did not feel treasured by someone important in their life. Maybe they did not receive proper physical touch, or they were abused. Perhaps they did not develop authentic, deep, meaningful relationships with loved ones. Maybe they never received unconditional love. Or, possibly they actually received all these things, but they've still been living with an orphan spirit without even realizing it—it has become a way of life, a habit that is hard to break.

These habits cause us to search for acceptance, significance, and identity in all the wrong places. We begin to seek the approval and praise of man. We may feel a deep need to be recognized for our service or for the things we do. We may develop critical attitudes, blame others, harbor jealousy, or become easily offended by leadership or those we are supposed to submit under.

A Comparison of the Heart of an Orphan to the Heart of Sonship
The **heart of an orphan** is rooted in insecurity, striving, and self-reliance. It constantly seeks validation and significance outside of the Father's love. In contrast, the **heart of sonship** rests in the love of the Father, knowing that we are entirely accepted, fully loved, and fully secure in our identity as His children. The journey from an orphan spirit to mature sonship is a transformational process of aligning our hearts with the Father's heart, understanding His love, and living out of that place of deep, abiding relationship.

The **Divine Handshake** invites us into this profound relationship with God, where we move from servants to friends and from friends to sons and daughters. As we embrace this journey, may we break free from the orphan spirit, walk in our true identity, and live as mature sons and daughters who reflect the heart of our Heavenly Father to a world desperately in need of His love.

Overcoming the Orphan Mindset: Embracing Sonship in the Father's Love

The **orphan mindset** is a spiritual condition rooted in feelings of abandonment, rejection, and a lack of belonging. It drives individuals to live as if they have no home, no inheritance, and no secure identity in the Father's love. To overcome the orphan mindset, one must embark on a journey of transformation—a journey from alienation to acceptance, from striving to rest, and from insecurity to security in God's love. This process involves several key steps, each grounded in biblical truths and empowered by the Holy Spirit.

1. **Embrace the Spirit of Adoption**

The first and most crucial step in overcoming the orphan mindset is to **embrace the Spirit of adoption**. When we are born again, we receive not just salvation but a new identity as sons and daughters of God. The Apostle Paul writes in **Romans 8:15**,

"The Spirit you received does not make you slaves so that you live in fear again; rather, the Spirit you received brought about your adoption to sonship. And by him we cry, 'Abba, Father.'"

This passage highlights that we have been adopted into God's family and have the privilege of calling Him "Abba," a term of deep intimacy meaning "Daddy" or "Papa." Embracing the Spirit of adoption means accepting that we are no longer spiritual orphans but beloved children with full access to the Father's heart and resources. It means living from a place of knowing that we are unconditionally loved, accepted, and valued by God.

2. Renew Your Mind with the Truth of God's Word

Overcoming the orphan mindset requires a **renewing of the mind**. The orphan mindset is often filled with lies—lies of unworthiness, abandonment, fear, and insecurity. To counter these lies, we must fill our minds with the **truth of God's Word**. The Bible is filled with promises and affirmations of our identity as God's children. Scriptures such as **Ephesians 1:5** remind us,

> *"He predestined us for adoption to sonship through Jesus Christ, in accordance with his pleasure and will."*

Regularly meditating on and declaring Scriptures that affirm our identity as sons and daughters can help transform our thinking. As we align our thoughts with God's truth, we begin to see ourselves as He sees us—loved, chosen, and secure. This renewed mindset helps break down the strongholds of fear, rejection, and inadequacy that the orphan spirit perpetuates.

3. Cultivate Intimacy with the Father

Intimacy with God is vital to overcoming the orphan mindset. Many believers struggle with feeling like orphans because they lack a deep, personal relationship with the Father. Jesus emphasized the importance of intimacy in **John 15:15** when He said,

> *"I no longer call you servants because a servant does not know his master's business. Instead, I have called you friends, for everything that I learned from my Father I have made known to you."*

Cultivating intimacy with God involves spending time in His presence through prayer, worship, and the study of His Word. It means learning to listen to His voice and resting in His love. As we draw near to Him, we experience His love in more profound and more personal ways. This intimate relationship is what assures us that we are not orphans but sons and daughters who are deeply known and fully loved by our Heavenly Father.

4. **Break Agreement with Lies and Strongholds**

An orphan mindset is often sustained by **agreements with lies** that the enemy has sown into our lives. These lies may sound like, "I am not enough," "I am not loved," or "I must perform to be accepted." To overcome the orphan mindset, we must **renounce** and **break agreement** with these lies. **2 Corinthians 10:4-5** reminds us,

> *"The weapons we fight with are not the weapons of the world. On the contrary, they have the divine power to demolish strongholds. We demolish arguments and every pretension that sets itself up against the knowledge of God, and we take captive every thought to make it obedient to Christ."*

Breaking agreements with lies involves confessing them, repenting for believing them, and replacing them with the truth of God's Word. For example, instead of agreeing with the lie, "I am not enough," declare, "I am fearfully and wonderfully made" (**Psalm 139:14**). Instead of, "I must perform to be accepted," declare, "I am accepted in the Beloved" (**Ephesians 1:6**). These declarations help to dismantle the strongholds of the orphan spirit and establish a foundation of truth.

5. **Seek Healing from Past Wounds**

The orphan mindset often takes root in past **wounds** of rejection, abandonment, or neglect. To overcome this mindset, it is essential to seek healing from these wounds. This may involve a process of **forgiving** those who have hurt or abandoned us, releasing bitterness and resentment, and allowing the Holy Spirit to minister to the deep places of our hearts.

Jesus came to heal the brokenhearted and set the captives free (**Luke 4:18**). Part of this healing process is inviting the Holy Spirit to reveal any hidden wounds and lies that need to be addressed. It may also involve seeking out godly counsel or participating in inner healing ministries that can guide us through the journey of healing and restoration.

6. Develop a Heart of Sonship through Spiritual Disciplines

Developing a **heart of sonship** involves embracing spiritual disciplines that help us grow in our relationship with God and reinforce our identity as His children. These disciplines include **prayer, worship, fasting, Bible study, and fellowship** with other believers.

Prayer and worship draw us closer to the Father, reinforcing our identity as His children. Fasting helps us to deny the flesh and align our desires with God's. Regular study of the Bible renews our minds with the truth, while fellowship with other believers provides accountability and encouragement. Together, these disciplines help cultivate a mindset of sonship and dependence on the Father.

7. Embrace Spiritual Community and Accountability

The orphan spirit often thrives in isolation. One of the keys to overcoming this mindset is to **embrace spiritual community** and seek **accountability**. God created us for relationships, and it is within the Body of Christ that we find encouragement, support, and accountability. In a healthy spiritual community, we can experience the love of the Father through our brothers and sisters in Christ. We are reminded that we are not alone and that we belong to a family.

Hebrews 10:24-25 encourages us,

"And let us consider how we may spur one another on toward love and good deeds, not giving up meeting together, as some are in the habit of doing, but encouraging one another—and all the more as you see the Day approaching."

Being part of a spiritual community helps us to grow in our identity as sons and daughters. It provides a safe place to be vulnerable, to share our struggles, and to receive encouragement and correction. Through this community, we learn to walk in our true identity and overcome the lies of the orphan spirit.

8. Receive the Father's Love and Affirmation Daily

To overcome the orphan mindset, we must make it a daily practice to **receive the Father's love and affirmation**. This involves intentionally opening our hearts to God's love and allowing His Spirit to speak truth and affirmation over us. The more we position ourselves to receive His love, the more we become rooted in our identity as His children.

In **Romans 8:16**, we read,

"The Spirit himself testifies with our spirit that we are God's children."

This ongoing testimony of the Spirit is what grounds us in sonship and frees us from the orphan mindset. Regularly asking the Holy Spirit to reveal the Father's heart to us, to show us His love and affection, and to affirm our identity in Christ is essential for overcoming the orphan spirit.

9. Serve from a Place of Love, Not Obligation

One of the defining characteristics of an orphan spirit is the tendency to serve God and others from a place of obligation, striving, or a need to prove one's worth. To break free from this mindset, it is essential to learn to **serve from a place of love**—knowing that we are already fully accepted and loved by the Father. This shift in perspective allows us to serve with joy, freedom, and grace, rather than from a place of performance or fear.

Galatians 5:13 reminds us,

"You, my brothers and sisters, were called to be free. But do not use your freedom to indulge the flesh; rather, serve one another humbly in love."

Serving from a place of love reflects our understanding that we are secure in the Father's heart. It allows us to minister out of the overflow of His love rather than out of a sense of duty or fear of rejection.

10. Be Transformed by the Holy Spirit

Finally, overcoming the orphan mindset is a **work of the Holy Spirit**. It is not something we can accomplish on our own through self-effort. We must rely on the Holy Spirit to transform our hearts, renew our minds, and lead us into deeper intimacy with the Father. As we yield to the Spirit's work in our lives, He empowers us to walk in the fullness of our identity as sons and daughters of God.

2 Corinthians 3:18 declares,

"And we all, who with unveiled faces contemplate the Lord's glory, are being transformed into his image with ever-increasing glory, which comes from the Lord, who is the Spirit."

This transformation is ongoing and requires a posture of surrender and dependence on God. It is through the Holy Spirit that we are continually reminded of our sonship and equipped to live in the freedom and fullness of the Father's love.

From Orphans to Sons and Daughters

Overcoming the orphan mindset is a journey of deep healing, transformation, and renewal. It is about moving from a place of alienation to belonging, from striving to rest, and from insecurity to security in God's love. As we embrace our identity as sons and daughters, cultivate intimacy with the Father, and break agreement with the lies of the orphan spirit, we step into the fullness of what it means to be heirs of God and co-heirs with Christ. This journey is not just for our own healing but also for the healing of the world around us. As we grow in our identity as mature sons and daughters, we become carriers of the Father's love, bringing His kingdom to earth through the **Divine Handshake**.

Living as Sons and Daughters: Our Call to Manifest the Father's Heart

The journey from an orphan mindset to a heart of sonship is not only transformative for our personal lives, but it also has a profound impact on the world. **Romans 8:19** states,

> *"For the creation waits in eager expectation for the children of God to be revealed."*

Creation itself is longing for the manifestation of mature sons and daughters of God—those who live in the fullness of their identity, who reflect the heart of the Father, and who walk in the authority and purpose given to them. When we break free from the orphan spirit and embrace our true identity, we become potent ambassadors of God's kingdom, releasing His love, peace, and righteousness wherever we go.

The Role of Spiritual Fathers and Mothers in Overcoming the Orphan Spirit

Breaking the orphan spirit often requires the presence of **spiritual fathers and mothers**—those who have walked the journey of sonship themselves and are now able to guide others. Spiritual parents help to model the love of the Father, provide guidance, and speak life and identity over those struggling with feelings of abandonment or rejection.

Paul exemplifies this role in his letters to the early church, such as when he writes to the Corinthians in **1 Corinthians 4:15**:

> *"For though you have countless guides in Christ, you do not have many fathers. For I became your father in Christ Jesus through the gospel."*

Spiritual fathers and mothers are essential in helping believers move from an orphan mentality to one of mature sonship. They help to **affirm identity**, break off lies, and provide a safe environment for growth and healing. The presence of spiritual parenting is crucial for cultivating a culture where the orphan spirit is not just broken but replaced with the fullness of sonship.

Cultivating a Culture of Sonship in the Church

To truly overcome the orphan spirit, it is essential to cultivate a culture of **sonship** within our churches and communities. This culture should be characterized by love, acceptance, affirmation, and empowerment. The church must be a place where people feel safe to be vulnerable, where they can experience the Father's love through others, and where they are encouraged to grow in their identity as sons and daughters.

A culture of sonship is marked by **honor**—honor for God, for spiritual authority, and for one another. It is a culture where people are encouraged to see themselves as God sees them, to embrace their God-given identity, and to walk in their unique calling. In such a culture, the orphan spirit cannot thrive because the atmosphere is filled with the love and presence of God.

Galatians 4:6-7 reminds us,

"Because you are his sons, God sent the Spirit of his Son into our hearts, the Spirit who calls out, 'Abba, Father.' So you are no longer a slave but God's child, and since you are his child, God has made you also an heir."

This revelation of sonship should permeate every aspect of our church life, from our worship and teaching to our relationships and ministries. As we cultivate this culture, we create an environment where people are set free from the orphan mindset and step into the fullness of who they are in Christ.

The Divine Handshake: From Fear to Freedom

The **Divine Handshake** symbolizes the partnership and cooperation between God and His children. It is a picture of us joining hands with the Father, walking in step with Him, and working alongside Him to bring heaven to earth. When we understand and embrace this partnership, we move from a place of fear and striving to a place of freedom and purpose.

The orphan spirit keeps us bound in fear—fear of failure, fear of rejection, fear of not being enough. But when we embrace the **Divine Handshake** and live as sons and daughters, we enter a place of divine security and confidence. We know that we are loved, accepted, and equipped by the Father to fulfill His purposes on earth.

2 Timothy 1:7 declares,

"For God has not given us a spirit of fear, but of power and of love and of a sound mind."

As we walk in the truth of our sonship, fear loses its grip on our lives. We no longer live as spiritual orphans, striving to prove our worth. Instead, we rest in the Father's love, knowing that He is with us, He is for us, and He has called us to partner with Him in His redemptive work.

The Power of Living as Sons and Daughters

The journey of overcoming the orphan spirit and embracing sonship is a journey into the very heart of God. It is about knowing who we are in Him and living from that place of identity and intimacy. As we walk this journey, we are transformed by His love, healed of our wounds, and empowered to live as mature sons and daughters who reflect the Father's heart to the world.

The **Anatomy of the Divine Handshake** teaches us that God has not only extended His hand to us but has also invited us into a relationship of deep intimacy, purpose, and partnership. As we break free from the orphan mindset, embrace our identity as sons and daughters, and cultivate a culture of sonship within our communities, we fulfill the Father's heart and bring His kingdom to earth.

May we all step into the fullness of our calling as sons and daughters of God, co-laboring with Him to see His will be done on earth as it is in heaven.

The Impact of Mature Sonship: Manifesting the Kingdom on Earth

Mature sonship is not merely about understanding our identity as children of God; it is about stepping into the fullness of that identity and living it out in every area of our lives. When we embrace mature sonship, we begin to walk in a profound alignment with the Father's heart, purpose, and authority. This transformation has a far-reaching impact—personally, corporately within the church, and globally. Mature sons and daughters are catalysts for change, carriers of God's presence, and ambassadors of His kingdom on earth.

1. A Deeper Revelation of the Father's Heart

The first and most profound impact of mature sonship is a **deeper revelation of the Father's heart**. Mature sons and daughters move beyond the superficial understanding of God as a distant or transactional deity; they know Him as a loving Father who desires intimacy, relationship, and partnership with His children. This revelation transforms how they see God, themselves, and others.

In **John 15:15**, Jesus says,

"I no longer call you servants because a servant does not know his master's business. Instead, I have called you friends, for everything that I learned from my Father I have made known to you."

This scripture shows that mature sons and daughters have access to the Father's secrets. They understand His ways, His desires, and His plans because they walk closely with Him. This intimate relationship empowers them to pray and act according to the Father's will, bringing heaven to earth through their lives.

2. Walking in Authority and Power

Mature sonship carries with it the weight of **authority and power**. When we are confident in our identity as sons and daughters of God, we understand that we are not just followers of Christ but also co-heirs with Him, empowered to carry out His will on earth. **Romans 8:17** declares, *"Now if we are children, then we are heirs—heirs of God and co-heirs with Christ if indeed we share in his sufferings in order that we may also share in his glory."*

This passage emphasizes that as heirs, we have been given authority to operate in the same power that raised Christ from the dead. Mature sons and daughters understand their authority in Christ and are not afraid to use it. They heal the sick, cast out demons, and speak life into dead situations because they know they carry the authority of heaven. They understand that they are not powerless but have been given the keys to the kingdom to bind and loose on earth as it is in heaven (**Matthew 16:19**).

3. A Life of Overflowing Love and Grace
Mature sonship leads to a life marked by **overflowing love and grace**. Sons and daughters who are rooted in the Father's love have no need to strive for approval or recognition from others; they are secure in their identity and live from a place of abundance rather than lack. This security allows them to love others freely, without conditions or fear of rejection.

1 John 4:18 states,

"There is no fear in love. But perfect love drives out fear because fear has to do with punishment. The one who fears is not made perfect in love."

Mature sons and daughters live in the reality of perfect love. They are not driven by fear but by a deep desire to reflect the Father's heart to the world. Their lives become a testimony of God's grace, kindness, and mercy, drawing others into the kingdom.

4. Establishing a Culture of Sonship in the Church
The impact of mature sonship extends beyond individual lives to the **corporate body of Christ**. When mature sons and daughters come together, they establish a culture of sonship within the church. This culture

is characterized by honor, humility, love, and unity. It is a place where people are valued not for what they do but for who they are in Christ.

A culture of sonship empowers individuals to step into their God-given callings and purposes. It nurtures spiritual gifts and encourages the free flow of the Holy Spirit. It breaks down walls of division, competition, and jealousy because sons and daughters know that they are all equally loved and valued by the Father. This creates an environment where revival can flourish, where miracles become commonplace, and where the church truly reflects the glory of God.

Ephesians 4:13 speaks to this,

"Until we all reach unity in the faith and in the knowledge of the Son of God and become mature, attaining to the whole measure of the fullness of Christ."

This verse highlights that mature sonship brings about unity and fullness in the body of Christ. It creates a strong, healthy, and vibrant church that is a powerful witness to the world.

5. Manifesting the Kingdom of God on Earth

Mature sons and daughters are called to **manifest the kingdom of God on earth**. They are the hands and feet of Jesus, carrying His presence wherever they go. They are not content to live passive, complacent lives; they are driven by a passion to see God's kingdom come and His will be done on earth as it is in heaven. This means engaging with the world around them, bringing light into darkness, and transforming culture through the power of the Holy Spirit.

Romans 8:19 reminds us,

"For the creation waits in eager expectation for the children of God to be revealed."

Creation itself is groaning for the manifestation of mature sons and daughters—those who will bring about the restoration of all things. Mature sons and daughters understand that they are not here merely to survive but to **thrive** and to bring the life and love of God to every sphere of society—be it business, education, government, arts, or family.

6. Breaking Generational Curses and Establishing Blessings

Mature sonship has the power to **break generational curses** and establish generational blessings. Sons and daughters who are secure in their identities are able to break free from the patterns of sin, fear, and dysfunction that may have plagued their families for generations. They bring healing and restoration not only to their own lives but to the lives of their children and future generations.

Galatians 3:13-14 states,

"Christ redeemed us from the curse of the law by becoming a curse for us… He redeemed us so that the blessing given to Abraham might come to the Gentiles through Christ Jesus so that by faith we might receive the promise of the Spirit."

Mature sons and daughters carry this generational blessing, passing it on to others. They are the ones who stand in the gap, interceding for their families, communities, and nations and breaking the power of the orphan spirit that has caused so much destruction. By living as mature sons and daughters, they pave the way for others to experience the fullness of God's love and purpose.

7. Living in Divine Partnership with God

Mature sonship is about living in a **divine partnership** with God. It is the essence of the **Divine Handshake**—a continuous, dynamic relationship where we walk hand in hand with the Father, co-laboring with Him to bring His plans and purposes to pass. Mature sons and daughters do not work for God out of obligation; they work with Him out of love. They understand that they are partners in His redemptive plan for humanity.

1 Corinthians 3:9 reminds us,

"For we are co-workers in God's service; you are God's field, God's building."

This partnership is not a burden but a joy. It is a privilege to work alongside the Creator of the universe, to be His voice, His hands, and His feet on earth. Mature sons and daughters embrace this calling with passion, knowing that their lives are not their own but are part of a more remarkable story—God's story of redemption and restoration.

The Power of Mature Sonship

The impact of mature sonship is far-reaching and transformative. It begins with a profound revelation of the Father's heart and leads to a life of authority, love, and power. It establishes a culture of sonship within the church, manifests the kingdom of God on earth, breaks generational curses, and creates a divine partnership with God. As mature sons and daughters, we are called to be carriers of His glory, ambassadors of His kingdom, and reflections of His love.

When we embrace mature sonship, we step into our divine destiny. We are no longer bound by the orphan spirit but are free to live as heirs of God, co-heirs with Christ, and instruments of His kingdom on earth. This is the power of the **Divine Handshake**—a life fully aligned with the Father, fully empowered by His Spirit, and fully committed to His mission.

CHAPTER 8

The Framework of the Divine Handshake

The concept of the **Divine Handshake** is a profound expression of God's relational and purposeful engagement with humanity. It is the idea that we, as believers, are invited into a co-laboring relationship with God, where our relationship with Him fuels our purpose, and our purpose is rooted in His divine will. This framework, as outlined in the Lord's Prayer (Luke 11:2-4), serves as a robust template for our daily walk with God, emphasizing paternity, position, praise, purpose, provision, propitiation, and protection.

To fully embrace and strengthen this framework, we need to delve deeply into each component, understanding its significance, applying it practically, and recognizing how it transforms our relationship with God and our role in His Kingdom.

1. Understanding Paternity: Our Father

The very first line of the Lord's Prayer, "Our Father in Heaven," sets the tone for the entire prayer. It establishes the nature of our relationship with God—one of **paternity**. This is not just a religious term but a foundational truth that changes everything. God is not a distant deity, an impersonal force, or an unreachable authority; He is **Father**. Understanding God as Father reshapes our approach to Him from fear and formality to intimacy and trust.

In **Malachi 4:6**, it is written, "He will turn the hearts of the fathers to their children, and the hearts of the children to their fathers." This prophetic word speaks to the relational restoration that God desires between Himself and His people. Before we can fulfill our divine purpose, we must first understand and embrace our identity as His children.

I remember growing up with a skewed perspective of God. I thought of Him as this stern judge waiting to catch me in a mistake. It wasn't until I had a profound encounter with His love that I realized He was a Father yearning to be in a relationship with me. This shift transformed my prayer life. Instead of coming to Him out of duty or fear, I began to approach Him with confidence, knowing that I am His son, and He delights in me. This understanding of **paternity** is critical for any believer. It is the bedrock of our faith. When we truly see God as our Father, we find security, significance, and identity.

2. **Embracing Our Position: Seated in Heavenly Places**

The phrase "Our Father in Heaven" also speaks to our **position**. Understanding our position in Christ is pivotal for living out the divine handshake. We are not mere beggars on earth hoping for a morsel of grace; we are **seated in heavenly places with Christ** (**Ephesians 2:6**). This changes how we approach prayer, challenges, and life itself. We are not fighting for victory but from victory. Our spiritual position grants us authority.

In practical terms, this means that our prayers are not mere wishes thrown into the wind. They are declarations backed by the authority of heaven. When we understand that we are positioned in Christ, it emboldens our faith. I've seen this shift in my own life. There was a time when I would pray timidly, almost as if I were trying not to disturb God. But when I grasped that I was seated with Christ, my prayers became bold and confident. I began to pray with the authority of a son, not the hesitation of a stranger.

3. The Power of Praise: Hallowed Be Your Name

The next component of the divine framework is **praise**—"Hallowed be your name." Praise is the key to entering God's presence and experiencing His power. **Psalm 100:4** teaches us to "Enter his gates with thanksgiving, and his courts with praise." Praise is more than just singing songs; it is a spiritual weapon that brings heaven to earth.

Praise enthrones God in our circumstances. As stated in **Psalm 22:3**, "You are holy, enthroned on the praises of Israel." When we praise, we are not merely expressing gratitude; we are inviting God's rulership and authority into our lives. Think of it like this: praise is the highway that leads us into the throne room of God. It shifts our focus from our problems to His power.

I remember facing a significant challenge in ministry. The weight of leadership and decision-making was overwhelming, and I felt cornered on all sides. During that time, God taught me the power of praise. Instead of focusing on the issues, I began to praise God intentionally. As I did, I felt a shift—not in my circumstances, but in my perspective. God became more extensive, and my problems became smaller. This is the power of praise; it aligns us with heaven's reality and brings God's authority to bear on our earthly struggles.

4. Living with Purpose: Your Kingdom Come, Your Will Be Done

"Your kingdom come, your will be done, on earth as it is in heaven." This line from the Lord's Prayer is a clarion call to **purpose**. Everything in the Kingdom of God revolves around purpose. We were not created randomly; we were **designed with a divine assignment**. We are here to bring heaven to earth, to manifest God's will in our lives, families, communities, and nations.

Romans 12:2 reminds us, "Do not conform to the pattern of this world but be transformed by the renewing of your mind. Then you will be able to test and approve what God's will is—his good, pleasing, and perfect will." Knowing God's will is not a mysterious quest; it is a process of transformation. When we align our minds and hearts with His, we begin to understand and live out His purpose.

For many years, I struggled with this concept. I thought God's will was this elusive, hidden treasure I had to find. But as I deepened my relationship with Him, I realized that His will is not hidden; it is revealed through intimacy and alignment with His Word. I discovered my purpose was not about doing great things for God but about being in a relationship with Him and letting His greatness flow through me.

5. Trusting in Provision: Give Us This Day Our Daily Bread

Provision is a fundamental aspect of the divine handshake. "Give us this day our daily bread" teaches us to trust God for **daily provision**. This is more than just physical sustenance; it encompasses spiritual, emotional, and relational provision. God is our provider, but His provision is tied to our obedience and alignment with His will.

Many believers want provision without purpose. They want God to bless them abundantly without understanding the vision He has for their lives. But provision follows vision. When we align with God's purpose, His provision flows naturally. In my life, I've seen this principle at work countless times. When I sought God for provision without clarity of purpose, I often found myself frustrated and anxious. But when I aligned with His vision, provision flowed effortlessly.

6. Practicing Propitiation: Forgive Us Our Sins, as We Forgive Others

"Forgive us our sins, for we also forgive everyone who is indebted to us." Here, we see the principle of **propitiation** or atonement. Forgiveness is at the heart of the gospel and the framework of the divine handshake. Our relationship with God is only possible because of His forgiveness toward us, and in turn, we must extend that forgiveness to others.

Unforgiveness is a significant hindrance in our walk with God. It blocks the flow of grace and disrupts the divine handshake. In **Matthew**

6:14, Jesus said, "For if you forgive other people when they sin against you, your Heavenly Father will also forgive you." Forgiveness is not optional; it is a command and a prerequisite for answered prayers.

I've witnessed this truth in action many times. There were seasons in my life when I harbored unforgiveness, and I noticed a distinct lack of peace and clarity. But when I chose to forgive, even those who deeply hurt me, I felt a release in my spirit. Forgiveness opens the door for God's healing, restoration, and blessing. It is essential to the divine framework.

7. Guarding Against Temptation: Lead Us Not into Temptation, but Deliver Us from Evil

"Lead us not into temptation, but deliver us from evil." This final line of the Lord's Prayer speaks to **protection**. In our journey of faith, there will be temptations and trials. But God promises to guide us and provide a way of escape. **1 Corinthians 10:13** states, "No temptation has overtaken you except what is common to mankind. And God is faithful; he will not let you be tempted beyond what you can bear."

To strengthen the framework of the divine handshake, we must remain vigilant. The enemy's goal is to disrupt our relationship with God and our fulfillment of His purpose. But God has given us spiritual armor, His Word, and His Spirit to guard against the schemes of the enemy.

There was a time in my ministry when I faced intense spiritual warfare. Temptations to quit, doubt, and fear were relentless. But God taught me to rely on His Word and to stand firm in prayer. I realized that God doesn't permanently remove the battle, but He equips us to stand in it. Deliverance comes not by avoidance but by facing the enemy with the whole armor of God.

8. Building Intimacy through Daily Devotion

The divine handshake requires ongoing **intimacy with God**. Our relationship with God must be cultivated daily through prayer, worship, and time in His Word. This is where the divine framework is genuinely strengthened. Daily devotion keeps our hearts tender and our spirits aligned with His.

I often tell people that the most essential part of my day is the time I spend with God. It is in those quiet moments that I hear His voice, senses His direction, and receive His peace. When we neglect daily intimacy, we risk drifting from His purpose and losing sight of His presence. The Lord's Prayer is not just a formula; it is a daily rhythm that anchors us in God's reality.

9. Engaging in Co-Laboring with God

The essence of the **divine handshake** is co-laboring with God. We are not called to work for God but to work **with Him**. This partnership is beautifully illustrated in **2 Corinthians 6:1**, "We appeal to you not to receive the grace of God in vain." God's grace is given not for us to sit idle but to engage actively in His Kingdom's work.

There is nothing more fulfilling than knowing you are working in partnership with God. Whether in ministry, business, or daily life, knowing that you are co-laboring with Him brings purpose and joy. I remember a time when I tried to do everything in my strength. The result was burnout and frustration. But when I learned to co-labor with God, everything changed. His grace, wisdom, and strength flowed effortlessly, and I found a rhythm of rest and productivity.

10. Continuous Growth and Spiritual Maturity

Finally, the framework of the divine handshake requires **continuous growth**. We must always be learning, growing, and maturing in our faith. As the Apostle Paul said in **Philippians 3:13-14**, "Forgetting what is behind and straining toward what is ahead, I press on toward the goal to win the prize for which God has called me heavenward in Christ Jesus."

Growth happens in the context of community, discipleship, and personal commitment to pursue God. The more we grow, the more our understanding of the divine handshake deepens, and our ability to walk in His purpose expands.

Strengthening the Framework of the Divine Handshake

The **Divine Handshake framework**—God's relational partnership with us to bring His Kingdom on earth as it is in heaven—provides a robust structure for living out our faith. Yet, like any framework, it requires continuous strengthening, alignment, and attention to be fully effective. Strengthening this divine framework involves deepening our understanding, refining our practices, and aligning our hearts with God's will in every aspect of our lives.

1. **Deepening Understanding of the Framework**

To strengthen the framework, we must first deepen our understanding of its foundational elements. The **Lord's Prayer** outlines the core components: paternity, position, praise, purpose, provision, propitiation, and protection. Each element is essential to the overall structure, and each must be fully grasped and lived out.

Paternity:
Recognize God as the **Father**. Strengthen this by cultivating intimacy with Him. This involves moving beyond a transactional relationship into a transformational one, where we seek His presence more than His presence. Understanding that we are sons and daughters, not just servants, changes our approach to prayer, worship, and obedience.

Position:
Acknowledge our **position in Christ**. Our authority is not based on our own merit but on our position in heavenly places with Christ. This requires a renewal of the mind, as stated in **Romans 12:2**. To strengthen this, continually remind yourself of your identity and authority in Christ, not based on feelings but on the truth of God's Word.

Praise:
Reinforce the practice of **praise**. Praise isn't just the songs we sing but a lifestyle of honoring God in all things. Strengthen this by daily choosing gratitude, even in difficult circumstances. Praise enthrones God and aligns our hearts with His sovereignty.

Purpose:
Clarify your **purpose** in God's plan. Strengthen this by seeking clarity in your divine assignment and calling. Engage in spiritual disciplines like fasting, prayer, and meditating on the Word to discern God's specific purpose for your life.

Provision, Propitiation, and Protection:
These components depend on understanding God's provision through obedience, His forgiveness through grace, and His protection through trust. Strengthen them by living a life of humility, repentance, and dependence on God.

2. **Cultivating Spiritual Disciplines**

The strength of the **Divine Handshake** framework is directly related to the **strength of our spiritual disciplines**. The more consistent and intentional we are in our spiritual practices, the more robust the framework becomes.

Prayer and Meditation:
True prayer is not just about speaking but also about listening and aligning our hearts with God's heart. To strengthen the framework, make prayer a daily priority, not just a ritual but an intimate conversation with God. Meditate on His Word, allowing it to shape and renew your mind.

Worship and Praise:
Make worship a lifestyle, not an event. Engage in both corporate worship with other believers and private worship in your personal time with God. Worship moves the heart of God and aligns us with His purposes.

Fasting and Repentance:
These practices keep us humble and remind us of our dependence on God. Fasting breaks the hold of the flesh and realigns us with the Spirit. Regular repentance keeps our hearts pure and sensitive to God's leading.

Community and Fellowship:
The framework of the Divine Handshake is not meant to be walked alone. **Hebrews 10:25** reminds us not to forsake gathering together. Community strengthens us, holds us accountable, and provides encouragement and correction.

3. Aligning Our Lives with Kingdom Priorities

To strengthen the framework, we must align our lives more closely with Kingdom priorities. This involves reordering our values, decisions, and actions to reflect God's heart and mission.

Kingdom First Mindset:
Jesus taught us to seek first the Kingdom of God (**Matthew 6:33**). This means prioritizing God's will, not our own, in every area of life—finances, relationships, career, and ministry. Evaluate your life regularly: Are your priorities in line with God's Kingdom?

Stewardship and Obedience:
Strengthen the framework by being a faithful steward of what God has given you—your time, talents, and resources. Obedience is better than sacrifice (**1 Samuel 15:22**). When God asks something of you, obey without delay.

Forgiveness and Reconciliation:
Offenses can weaken the framework, as they cause division and hinder our prayers. To strengthen it, practice forgiveness daily. Live in a state of grace, as Jesus taught, "Forgive us our debts, as we also have forgiven our debtors" (**Matthew 6:12**).

4. **Guarding the Gates of the Framework**
The **framework of the Divine Handshake** involves a spiritual gate—an access point between heaven and earth. To keep this gate open and the framework strong, we must guard against anything that would hinder the flow of God's presence and power.

Watchfulness and Vigilance:
Jesus warned His disciples to "watch and pray" (**Matthew 26:41**). Strengthen the framework by being spiritually alert. Watch for distractions, deceptions, and temptations that can weaken your commitment to God's purpose.

Spiritual Warfare:
Understand that we have an enemy who seeks to disrupt the framework. **Ephesians 6:12** tells us that we wrestle not against flesh and blood but against principalities and powers. Strengthen the framework by putting on the whole armor of God and engaging in spiritual warfare when necessary.

Holiness and Purity:
1 Peter 1:16 calls us to be holy as God is holy. Holiness strengthens the framework by ensuring there are no breaches where the enemy can enter. Keep your heart pure, your motives clean, and your actions righteous.

5. Embracing Continuous Growth and Learning

The **Divine Handshake** is not static but dynamic. It grows stronger as we grow deeper in our relationship with God and our understanding of His Word.

Lifelong Learning:

Be a student of the Word. The more you know God's Word, the better you understand His will and ways. Study Scripture diligently and let it be the foundation upon which you build your life.

Mentorship and Discipleship:

To strengthen the framework, find mentors and be a mentor to others. Discipleship enhances the community and helps believers grow in their faith and understanding of God's purposes.

Openness to Correction:

Proverbs 12:1 reminds us that whoever loves discipline loves knowledge, but whoever hates correction is stupid. Strengthen the framework by being open to correction and humble enough to change when needed.

6. Engaging in Active Co-Laboring with God

To strengthen the framework, we must actively engage in **co-laboring with God**. This involves moving beyond passive Christianity into active partnership with God's mission on earth.

Serve in Your Local Church:

Strengthen the framework by finding ways to serve within your local church or community. Whether it's through prayer, teaching, hospitality, or evangelism, your service matters in God's Kingdom.

Evangelism and Outreach:
The framework is strengthened as we share the Gospel and disciple others. The Great Commission (**Matthew 28:19-20**) is not optional but essential to fulfilling our divine purpose.

Faith in Action:
Strengthen the framework by putting your faith into action. **James 2:17** states that faith without works is dead. Live out your faith in practical, tangible ways that reflect God's love and truth.

7. Trusting in God's Timing and Sovereignty

Finally, strengthening the framework means trusting in God's timing and sovereignty. We are not building our kingdom; we are partnering with God to create His.

Patience and Perseverance:
Hebrews 6:12 encourages us to imitate those who, through faith and patience, inherit the promises. Strengthen the framework by developing patience and trusting God's timing.

Faith Over Fear:
Challenges and trials will come, but God's purposes will prevail. Strengthen the framework by choosing faith over fear, trusting that God is faithful to complete the work He has begun in you (**Philippians 1:6**).

The Ongoing Strengthening of the Divine Framework

Strengthening the framework of the **Divine Handshake** is an ongoing process of growth, alignment, and active participation in God's Kingdom. It requires intentional effort to deepen our understanding, cultivate spiritual disciplines, align our lives with Kingdom priorities, guard against spiritual breaches, embrace continuous growth, and actively co-labor with God.

As we strengthen this framework, we become effective vessels for His Kingdom, bringing heaven to earth and fulfilling our divine purpose with joy, authority, and power.

CHAPTER 9

Heaven's Invitation— Stepping into the Divine Handshake

God's Kingdom is not a distant place far beyond the stars, nor is it an abstract concept that merely exists in our minds. It is a reality that God invites us to experience and manifest here on earth. When Jesus spoke of the Kingdom of Heaven, He was not speaking of a faraway dream but of a present reality that is accessible to us right now. In this chapter, we delve into the profound concept of "Heaven's Invitation»— an invitation that calls us to shift our perspective, embrace a Kingdom mindset, and operate under an open heaven. This invitation is intrinsically connected to the Divine Handshake, where heaven meets earth, and God partners with His people to bring His purposes to pass.

The Invitation from Heaven: A Call to a Higher Perspective
In **Mark 1:9-10**, we read about a pivotal moment in Jesus' life. Jesus comes from Nazareth and is baptized by John in the Jordan River. "Just as Jesus was coming up out of the water, he saw heaven being torn open and the Spirit descending on him like a dove" (**Mark 1:10**). This was not just a symbolic act but a powerful declaration of an open heaven. The heavens were torn open for Jesus, and through Him, they remain open for us. This tearing of heaven was a violent act, a divine disruption signaling that heaven's resources, power, and presence are now available on earth.

A Shift in Perspective:
The tearing of heaven represents God's invitation for us to see things from His vantage point. God is saying, "Come up here! See things as I see them." It is not a call to change our physical location but to elevate our spiritual perspective. When we change our altitude in the spirit, our perspective shifts. Our vision becomes aligned with God's reality rather than our limited, earthly viewpoint.

Living Under an Open Heaven:
Jesus, our older brother, and example, modeled how to live under an open heaven. His life was marked by a continual awareness of heaven's realities. The Spirit descended on Him and remained on Him, empowering Him to fulfill His earthly ministry. Likewise, the Holy Spirit abides in us and comes upon us to achieve specific purposes. When we live in the awareness of an open heaven, we access divine wisdom, power, and resources for every situation we face.

The Dual Anointing of the Holy Spirit:
The Holy Spirit operates in us in two distinct ways: *in us* to continuously abide for daily living and i*n us* to accomplish specific tasks. The anointing within us cultivates our character, while the anointing upon us empowers us for ministry. God's invitation is for us to operate in both dimensions, fully utilizing the power of the Holy Spirit that resides in us.

Revelation's Open Door: The Invitation to Ascend

Revelation 4:1 provides another glimpse of Heaven's invitation: "After this I looked, and there before me was a door standing open in heaven. And the voice I had first heard speaking to me like a trumpet said, 'Come up here, and I will show you what must take place after this.'" This scripture paints a picture of an open door in heaven and a divine call to ascend higher.

An Invitation to See from Heaven's Perspective:
The call to "come up here" is an invitation to see beyond the natural and to understand the divine purposes that are unfolding. It is a call to see life's circumstances from God's perspective. When we accept this invitation, we move from a place of fear and uncertainty to a place of faith and clarity. We begin to operate from a position of victory rather than defeat.

Changing Altitude, Changing Attitude:
Our attitude towards life's challenges transforms as we ascend to God's perspective. When our attitude changes, our attitude changes. We no longer see obstacles as insurmountable but as opportunities for God's power to be displayed. We no longer react to the darkness around us but respond to the light of God within us. This shift empowers us to live boldly and confidently, knowing that we are in an open heaven.

Operating from a Kingdom Reality:
God's invitation is for us to operate from a Kingdom reality, where heaven's resources are available to us. This requires a change in perspective, moving from a natural mindset to a supernatural mindset. The Kingdom of God is not bound by earthly limitations; it operates in a realm where all things are possible. When we accept this invitation, we begin to see miracles, breakthroughs, and divine interventions as the norm rather than the exception.

The Power of an Open Heaven: Accessing Heaven's Resources

Living under an open heaven means that everything we need to live a life of fulfillment and purpose has already been provided. The key to accessing these heavenly resources is not in striving or begging but in understanding our position and perspective.

Understanding What We Already Possess:
When Jesus declared, "It is finished" on the cross, the veil in the temple was torn, giving us direct access to God's presence. The same word used for "torn" (schizō) is used to describe the heavens being torn open at Jesus' baptism. This violent tearing signifies that nothing can separate us from God's presence and resources. As believers, we must understand that we already live under an open heaven. We do not need to strive for what is already ours; we need to believe and access it by faith.

Avoiding the Trap of Doubt and Unbelief:
When we pray for what we already have, we cancel what we already possess. When we continue to ask God for what He has already provided, we operate from a place of unbelief rather than faith. The enemy thrives on our ignorance. When we believe a lie, we empower the liar. Therefore, it is crucial to renew our minds with the truth of God's Word and operate from a place of understanding and authority.

Living Offensively, Not Defensively:
Many believers live in a defensive posture, reacting to the enemy's attacks rather than advancing God's Kingdom. Jesus modeled a different way. He did not react to the power of darkness but only responded to what the Father told Him. We are called to do the same. When we live in an open heaven, we are not merely trying to survive; we are called to invade the gates of hell with the power and authority of heaven.

Understanding the Concept of an Open Heaven

The concept of an "open heaven" is central to the Kingdom of God and is woven throughout Scripture. It is not merely a theological idea but a spiritual reality that has profound implications for how we live, pray, and minister. To expand on this, we need to explore what it means to live under an open heaven, how it impacts our lives, and what it requires of us as believers.

The Biblical Foundation of an Open Heaven

The term "open heaven" is used to describe a spiritual condition where there is unrestricted access to the heavenly realm. It signifies a state where the barriers between heaven and earth are removed, allowing for the free flow of God's presence, power, and provision. Several critical passages in the Bible highlight this concept:

Jesus' Baptism and the Tearing Open of Heaven:
In **Mark 1:9-10**, we read that as Jesus was baptized, "he saw heaven being torn open and the Spirit descending on him like a dove." This moment was significant because it marked the beginning of Jesus' public ministry under an open heaven. The word "torn" (Greek: *schizō*) implies a violent tearing or ripping apart, indicating that this was a decisive action by God to open heaven over His Son. This tearing open was not a gentle opening but a forceful breakthrough, symbolizing God's powerful intention to make His presence accessible to humanity.

The Rending of the Veil at the Crucifixion:
The same word, *schizō*, is used in **Matthew 27:51** to describe the tearing of the temple veil at the moment of Jesus' death: "At that moment the curtain of the temple was torn in two from top to bottom." This event symbolizes the removal of the separation between God and humanity. Through Jesus' sacrifice, heaven was permanently opened for those who believe in Him, granting direct access to the Father. This act made it possible for believers to enter into God's presence boldly, without the need for an earthly mediator.

Revelation of an Open Door in Heaven:
In **Revelation 4:1**, the Apostle John describes a vision where he saw "a door standing open in heaven" and a voice saying, "Come up here, and I will show you what must take place after this." This passage reveals that an open heaven provides access to divine revelation and insight into

God's plans and purposes. It invites believers to ascend to a higher level of spiritual perception, where they can see from God's perspective and understand His will more clearly.

Living Under an Open Heaven: The Believer's Reality

Living under an open heaven is not just for select individuals; it is the inheritance of every believer in Christ. When Jesus tore open the heavens, He did so for all who would follow Him, making it possible for every Christian to experience the fullness of God's presence, power, and purpose.

The Continual Presence of God:

An open heaven signifies the unceasing presence of God in our lives. Unlike in the Old Testament, where God's presence was often localized in specific places (like the Ark of the Covenant or the Temple), under an open heaven, His presence is accessible everywhere and at all times. This is why Jesus could promise, "And surely I am with you always, to the very end of the age" (**Matthew 28:20**). Believers can live with the awareness that God is always near, always available, and always willing to engage with them.

The Flow of Divine Resources:

Under an open heaven, there is a flow of divine resources—both spiritual and material. God's provision is not limited to finances or physical needs; it encompasses wisdom, revelation, strength, peace, joy, and more. **Philippians 4:19** states, "And my God will meet all your needs according to the riches of his glory in Christ Jesus." Living under an open heaven means having access to these riches and trusting that God's supply is limitless.

Empowerment for Kingdom Work:

When we live in an open heaven, we are empowered to fulfill God's purposes on earth. This empowerment comes through the Holy Spirit, who descended upon Jesus and now resides in every believer. **Acts 1:8** says,

"But you will receive power when the Holy Spirit comes on you; and you will be my witnesses." The power of the Holy Spirit is not just for personal edification but for mission. It equips us to preach the gospel, heal the sick, cast out demons, and advance the Kingdom of God wherever we go.

The Impact of an Open Heaven on Spiritual Warfare

Living under an open heaven profoundly affects how we engage in spiritual warfare. It changes our posture from one of defense to one of offense. When we understand that heaven is open over us, we realize that we are not fighting for victory; we are fighting from victory.

Authority Over the Enemy:
Jesus' death and resurrection disarmed the powers of darkness and gave believers authority over all the power of the enemy (**Colossians 2:15, Luke 10:19**). An open heaven means that this authority is readily accessible. We do not need to beg God for victory; we need to enforce the victory that Jesus has already won. This shifts our mindset from fear and insecurity to confidence and boldness.

Operating from a Higher Realm:
Spiritual warfare is often fought in the mind, where the enemy seeks to sow doubt, fear, and unbelief. However, when we live in an open heaven, our perspective is elevated. **Ephesians 2:6** tells us that we are "seated with him in the heavenly realms in Christ Jesus." This means that we are not fighting from a lowly position; we are fighting from a place of authority and dominion. Our prayers and declarations carry the weight of heaven's authority, and they can shift atmospheres and dismantle strongholds.

The Role of Faith in Warfare:
Living under an open heaven requires us to walk by faith and not by sight. Faith is the key to accessing the realities of an open heaven. When we pray, "Your kingdom come, Your will be done, on earth as it is in

heaven," we are declaring that the realities of heaven—peace, joy, healing, provision—are manifesting in our lives and in our world. **Hebrews 11:1** defines faith as "confidence in what we hope for and assurance about what we do not see." Even when circumstances look bleak, faith declares that heaven is open and God is working.

The Lifestyle of an Open Heaven: Characteristics and Requirements

Living under an open heaven is not automatic; it requires intentionality and commitment. There are certain characteristics and requirements for maintaining an open heaven over our lives.

A Lifestyle of Holiness and Obedience:
Holiness and obedience are non-negotiables for living under an open heaven. **Hebrews 12:14** says, "Without holiness, no one will see the Lord." Holiness is not about legalism but about alignment with God's character and purposes. Obedience, on the other hand, is the practical outworking of our faith. It is doing what God says, when He says it, and how He says it. When we walk in holiness and obedience, we stay under the open heaven and enjoy the blessings that come with it.

A Heart of Worship and Thanksgiving:
Worship is a powerful way to maintain an open heaven over our lives. Worship invites God's presence and creates an atmosphere where heaven and earth intersect. **Psalm 22:3** says, "But thou art holy, O thou that inhabitest the praises of Israel." When we worship, we enthrone God over our lives and situations, and we position ourselves to receive His direction and intervention. Thanksgiving is equally important because it acknowledges what God has done and positions us to receive more. **1 Thessalonians 5:18** says, "Give thanks in all circumstances; for this is God's will for you in Christ Jesus."

Engaging in Persistent Prayer and Intercession:

Prayer is the lifeline of living in an open heaven. It is through prayer that we access the resources of heaven and bring them to earth. **James 5:16** says, "The prayer of a righteous person is powerful and effective." Persistent prayer, coupled with faith, has the power to open heavens, break strongholds, and release God's will on earth. Intercession, which involves standing in the gap for others, is also crucial because it aligns our hearts with God's heart and His purposes for others.

A Spirit of Generosity and Stewardship:

Living under an open heaven is also marked by generosity and stewardship. God's resources flow to and through those who are willing to share them. **Proverbs 11:25** states, "A generous person will prosper; whoever refreshes others will be refreshed." Stewardship involves managing what God has entrusted to us—our time, talents, and treasures—in a way that honors Him and advances His Kingdom. When we are faithful stewards, God entrusts us with more and keeps the heavens open over us.

The Corporate Dimension of an Open Heaven

While living under an open heaven is a personal reality, it also has a corporate dimension. The church, as the body of Christ, is called to function under an open heaven and to operate in unity and power.

The Church as a Gate of Heaven:

In **Genesis 28:17**, Jacob had a dream where he saw a ladder reaching to heaven with angels ascending and descending on it. He declared, "This is none other than the house of God, and this is the gate of heaven." The church, as the house of God, is meant to be a gate of heaven where the presence of God is encountered, and His will is executed on earth. This requires the church to walk in unity, purity, and power.

Corporate Prayer and Worship as Keys to an Open Heaven:
When the church comes together in corporate prayer and worship, it creates an atmosphere for heaven to invade earth. **Acts 4:31** says, "After they prayed, the place where they were meeting was shaken. And they were all filled with the Holy Spirit and spoke the word of God boldly." The early church experienced open heavens because they prayed together, worshiped together, and moved in one accord.

The Role of Apostolic Leadership and Teaching:
Apostolic leadership and sound teaching are essential for maintaining an open heaven over a church or ministry. Apostolic leaders are called to equip the saints for the work of ministry and to release them into their God-given destinies. **Ephesians 4:11-12** states that God gave apostles, prophets, evangelists, pastors, and teachers "to equip his people for works of service, so that the body of Christ may be built up." Sound teaching helps believers understand their authority, identity, and inheritance in Christ, enabling them to live under an open heaven.

The Purpose of an Open Heaven: Advancing the Kingdom

Ultimately, the purpose of an open heaven is to advance the Kingdom of God on earth. It is about bringing heaven's realities—righteousness, peace, and joy in the Holy Spirit—into every sphere of influence.

Transforming Lives and Communities:
Under an open heaven, lives are transformed, and communities are impacted. The supernatural becomes natural, and miracles, signs, and wonders are a regular occurrence. **Mark 16:17-18** says, "And these signs will accompany those who believe: In my name, they will drive out demons; they will speak in new tongues… they will place their hands on sick people, and they will get well." When the church lives under an open heaven, the power of God flows freely, and people experience His love and power in tangible ways.

Demonstrating the Superiority of God's Kingdom:
Living under an open heaven allows believers to demonstrate the superiority of God's Kingdom over the kingdom of darkness. It reveals that the Kingdom of God is not just in word but in power (**1 Corinthians 4:20**). When we heal the sick, cast out demons, and preach the gospel with power, we show the world that the God we serve is alive, active, and able to save, heal, and deliver.

Preparing for the Return of Christ:
Finally, living under an open heaven prepares the church for the return of Christ. **Revelation 19:7** declares, "Let us rejoice and be glad and give him glory! For the wedding of the Lamb has come, and his bride has made herself ready." The open heaven over the church is a foretaste of the ultimate open heaven when Christ returns and establishes His reign on earth. Until then, we are called to live in such a way that reflects the reality of heaven on earth.

Embracing Heaven's Invitation

Heaven's invitation to live under an open heaven is an invitation to a higher way of living—a way marked by intimacy with God, empowerment by the Holy Spirit, and alignment with God's purposes. It is an invitation to partner with God in bringing heaven to earth and to live in the fullness of what Jesus paid for on the cross.

As we embrace this invitation, may we seek to cultivate lives of holiness, obedience, worship, prayer, generosity, and unity. May we steward the open heaven over us with wisdom and faithfulness, knowing that much is required of those to whom much is given? And may we, as the body of Christ, rise up to be an actual gate of heaven—a place where God's presence dwells, His voice is heard, and His Kingdom is advanced on earth as it is in heaven. This is our calling, our privilege, and our destiny.

God's Jealous Longing: Why He Invites Us to His World

God's invitation to live under an open heaven is driven by His jealous longing for His Spirit that dwells in us. **James 4:5** tells us, "Or do you think Scripture says without reason that he jealously longs for the spirit he has caused to dwell in us?"

A Holy Jealousy for Our Affection:
God is not jealous *of* us; He is jealous *for* us. He desires our wholehearted devotion and alignment with His purposes. He longs for His Spirit in us to be fully engaged in the divine partnership of bringing heaven to earth. When we live in alignment with God's will, we fulfill the purpose for which we were created.

Friendship with God vs. Friendship with the World:
The verse preceding this one, **James 4:4**, warns against friendship with the world, which makes us enemies of God. We cannot serve two masters. To live under an open heaven, we must fully commit ourselves to God's Kingdom and reject the world's systems and values. Our allegiance must be to God alone.

The Divine Handshake: Heaven's Invitation to Partnership:
The Divine Handshake is an invitation to partner with God in His redemptive plan for the world. It is an invitation to step into a higher reality where God's will is done on earth as it is in heaven. This partnership requires us to align our hearts, minds, and actions with God's purposes and to live from the reality of an open heaven.

Responding to the Invitation: Arising and Shining in a Dark World

Isaiah 60:1-2 speaks to us prophetically: "Arise, shine, for your light has come, and the glory of the Lord rises upon you. See, darkness covers the earth and thick darkness is over the peoples, but the Lord rises upon you and his glory appears over you."

A Call to Arise and Shine:
Even though darkness covers the earth, the light and glory of the Lord rise upon us. This is the time for the church to arise and shine. We are not to be overwhelmed by the darkness but to overcome it with the light of Christ. Heaven's invitation is for us to stand out, to be a beacon of hope, and to demonstrate the reality of an open heaven in our lives.

Walking in the Reality of an Open Heaven:
This prophecy was a messianic promise fulfilled in Jesus, and it remains a promise for us today. We live with an open invitation from God to walk under an open heaven. Heaven is waiting for us to mirror what happens in heaven. When we align our lives with heaven's realities, we become conduits of God's glory on earth.

Taking Responsibility for Our Spiritual Atmosphere:
We cannot wait for heaven to do something; heaven has already acted through Christ. Our role is to believe, understand, and walk in obedience. We rejoice, and then the atmosphere changes. We give, and heaven always provides. We engage the open invitation of an open heaven, and miracles happen. How we respond to heaven's invitation determines the spiritual atmosphere around us.

Stewarding the Power Within the Measure of Heaven's Response

Ephesians 3:20 declares, "Now to him who is able to do immeasurably more than all we ask or imagine, according to his power that is at work within us." The manifestation of an open heaven is directly tied to how we manage the power that God has entrusted to us.

The Principle of Stewardship:
God responds according to the power working within us. This means that there is a continuous open invitation for an open heaven, but it is accessed by how we steward His power. Jesus modeled perfect stewardship of an open heaven, and we are called to do the same.

Increasing Our Capacity for Heaven's Realities:
As we steward the power of God within us, we increase our capacity for more of heaven to manifest in our lives. The more we yield to the Holy Spirit, the more of heaven we experience. This involves a daily surrender to God's will, a commitment to live in purity and obedience, and a boldness to step out in faith.

Inviting Others to Experience an Open Heaven:
The concept of an open heaven is not just for our benefit; it is an invitation to others. We are called to create an atmosphere where others can encounter God's presence and power. An open heaven over our lives is meant to be a conduit for heaven to invade earth, transform lives, and advance God's Kingdom. As we live under this open heaven, we become carriers of His presence, ambassadors of His Kingdom, and instruments of His grace.

The Purpose of an Open Heaven: Invading the Gates of Hell

The ultimate goal of living under an open heaven is not to create a comfortable, spiritual experience for ourselves but to advance God's Kingdom by invading the gates of hell. Jesus said, "I will build my church, and the gates of Hades will not overcome it" (**Matthew 16:18**). This implies that the church, empowered by an open heaven, is not on the defensive but on the offensive.

The Church as a Force of Advancement:
The church is not a passive institution but an active, dynamic force. We are not called to retreat but to advance. An open heaven over our lives

means that we carry the authority and power of heaven wherever we go. We are called to challenge the status quo, push back the darkness, establish God's rule, and reign in every sphere of influence.

Engaging in Spiritual Warfare from a Place of Victory:
Spiritual warfare is not about fighting for victory but fighting from a place of victory. Jesus has already disarmed principalities and powers and made a public spectacle of them by triumphing over them through the cross (**Colossians 2:15**). Our role is to enforce that victory by living under an open heaven and using the authority given to us by Christ.

The Mission to Bring Heaven to Earth:
Our mandate is clear: "Your kingdom come, Your will be done, on earth as it is in heaven" (**Matthew 6:10**). This is not a passive prayer but a declaration of intent. It is a call to action for every believer to partner with God in manifesting His Kingdom on earth. The open heaven over our lives is an invitation to participate in this divine mission.

The Dynamics of Heaven's Invitation: Walking in Divine Partnership

Heaven's invitation is not just about experiencing spiritual highs; it is about walking in divine partnership with God. The Divine Handshake is a symbolic representation of this partnership, where heaven meets earth, and God partners with His people to fulfill His purposes.

The Divine Partnership Defined:
A partnership with God means we are not working *for* God but *with* God. We are co-laborers with Him (**1 Corinthians 3:9**), and this changes everything. When we realize that God is inviting us into His world to partner with Him, we stop striving and start thriving. We move from a place of performance to a place of presence.

Aligning with Heaven's Agenda:

To walk in divine partnership, we must align our lives with heaven's agenda. This means prioritizing God's will above our own and being sensitive to the leading of the Holy Spirit. It requires a commitment to prayer, worship, and the Word of God. As we align with heaven, we begin to see the manifestation of God's promises in our lives.

The Role of Faith in Divine Partnership:

Faith is the currency of heaven. It is impossible to please God without faith (**Hebrews 11:6**). Faith requires us to step out of our comfort zones and take risks. It means believing God's Word over our circumstances and trusting His promises even when things don't make sense. When we operate in faith, we align ourselves with heaven's realities and see the impossible become possible.

Transforming Earth with Heaven's Realities:
The Power of Agreement

One of the most powerful dynamics of Heaven's invitation is the principle of agreement. Jesus said, "Again, truly I tell you that if two of you on earth agree about anything they ask for, it will be done for them by my Father in heaven" (**Matthew 18:19**). Agreement on earth establishes what is in heaven.

The Power of Corporate Agreement:

There is a unique power that is released when believers come into agreement with heaven's agenda. This is why corporate prayer, worship, and fellowship are so important. When we gather together and agree on earth as it is in heaven, we create a spiritual atmosphere where God's presence can manifest powerfully. The early church understood this principle, and as a result, they "devoted themselves to the apostles' teaching and to fellowship, to the breaking of bread and to prayer" (**Acts 2:42**).

Unity in Diversity:
The body of Christ is made up of many parts, each unique and valuable. Our diversity is our strength, but it can also be a potential weakness if not handled correctly. True unity is not uniformity but harmony. It is when each part functions in its unique calling and gifting while being aligned with the whole. This kind of unity creates a powerful synergy that can transform communities and nations.

Creating an Atmosphere for Miracles:
When there is agreement in the Spirit, the atmosphere is ripe for miracles. Jesus often said, "Your faith has made you well" or "According to your faith let it be done to you" (**Matthew 9:22, 29**). Faith creates an atmosphere for heaven to invade Earth. When a community of believers comes together in faith, believing in the impossible, heaven responds.

Heaven's Response: Manifesting the Kingdom on Earth

The goal of living under an open heaven and accepting Heaven's invitation is to manifest the Kingdom of God on earth. This is not just about experiencing personal blessings but about transforming the world around us.

Kingdom Manifestation through Acts of Love and Power:
Jesus went about doing good and healing all who were oppressed by the devil (**Acts 10:38**). His life was marked by acts of love and power. As His followers, we are called to do the same. The open heaven over our lives is meant to be a source of blessing to others. We are called to feed the hungry, heal the sick, raise the dead, and preach the good news of the Kingdom.

Transforming Culture through Kingdom Values:
The Kingdom of God operates on a different set of values than the world. While the world values power, wealth, and influence, the Kingdom

values humility, servanthood, and love. As we live under an open heaven, we are called to model these Kingdom values in our workplaces, schools, communities, and homes. When we do, we become agents of transformation, bringing God's Kingdom to every sphere of society.

Partnering with Heaven in Intercession:
Prayer is one of the most potent ways we partner with heaven to bring about change on earth. When we pray, "Your kingdom come, Your will be done," we are not just making a wish but making a declaration. We are aligning our hearts with God's purposes and calling forth heaven's realities into our earthly situations. Intercession is about standing in the gap and contending for God's will to be done on earth as it is in heaven.

Stewarding an Open Heaven: A Sacred Responsibility

Living under an open heaven is a sacred responsibility that requires stewardship. At the end of the age, we will all be judged by how we managed the open heaven over our lives.

- **Managing the Power Within: Ephesians 3:20** reminds us that God is able to do immeasurably more than we can ask or imagine, but it is according to the power at work within us. This means that our experience of an open heaven is directly tied to how we manage the power and authority God has given us. We must be intentional in cultivating our relationship with God, walking in obedience, and exercising our faith.
- **Multiplying Heaven's Resources**: The parable of the talents (**Matthew 25:14-30**) teaches us the importance of multiplying what God has given us. Those who are faithful with little will be entrusted with more. Likewise, as we steward the open heaven over our lives, we can expect God to multiply His resources and increase His favor upon us.
- **The Impact of Stewardship on Generations**: The way we steward the open heaven over our lives will have a ripple effect on

future generations. Just as Jesus' life opened heaven for us, our lives can open heaven for others. We are called to leave a legacy of faith, obedience, and Kingdom impact that will continue to advance God's purposes long after we are gone.

Heaven's Invitation to All: A Call to Respond

Heaven's invitation is not a one-time event but a continual call to come up higher, to see from God's perspective, and to live under an open heaven. This invitation is available to every believer, but it requires a response.

Accepting the Invitation with Faith and Obedience:
To accept Heaven's invitation, we must step out in faith and obedience. It means letting go of our limited perspectives and embracing God's higher ways. It means living with an awareness of the open heaven over our lives and partnering with God to bring His Kingdom to earth.

Creating a Culture of Heaven on Earth:
As we accept this invitation, we are called to create a culture of heaven on earth. This is done through love, unity, service, and Kingdom advancement. The church is meant to be a reflection of heaven, a place where God's presence is tangible, His power is displayed, and His love is experienced.

Living as Heaven's Ambassadors:
Finally, we are called to live as Heaven's ambassadors, representing God's Kingdom wherever we go. An ambassador carries the authority and power of the one who sent them. As ambassadors of Christ, we have the authority and power of heaven. Our lives should reflect the realities of an open heaven and invite others to experience the same.

Heaven's invitation is clear: "Come up here!" Let us respond with a resounding "Yes, Lord!" and step into the fullness of what God has prepared for us. Let us live under an open heaven, steward His power within us, and partner with Him in bringing heaven to earth. This is the essence of the Divine Handshake—a partnership between heaven and earth that transforms lives, communities, and nations.

CHAPTER 10

The Bold Partnership—Making Big Plans with God

D.L. Moody's legacy in Christian ministry is not only a testament to his deep faith but also an inspiring example of what it means to co-labor with God under the power of a "divine handshake." Born to a poor family in Northfield, Massachusetts, Moody's journey to becoming a world-renowned evangelist was anything but straightforward. He started with little education, working as a shoe salesman before a pivotal encounter led him to Christ. This experience ignited a fire in his heart—a divine spark that propelled him into a life of bold faith and fearless action for the Kingdom of God.

Moody's philosophy of ministry can be encapsulated in his famous quote, "If God is your partner, make your plans big." This was not merely a catchphrase for him but a way of life. Moody believed that partnering with God demanded a faith that transcended human ability, logic, and comfort. He was known for his audacious initiatives, from founding the Moody Bible Institute to preaching to crowds of thousands across continents. Moody understood that the "divine handshake" between God and man was an invitation to expand our vision, stretch our faith, and embrace plans so large that only God could bring them to fruition.

The Power of Boldness in the Divine Handshake

To grasp the total weight of Moody's statement, we must understand the nature of boldness in our relationship with God. The Bible is filled with examples of God calling His people to boldness—boldness to conquer lands, to speak truth, and to live out His commands without fear. Proverbs 28:1 says:

"The wicked flee though no one pursues, but the righteous are as bold as a lion."

This boldness is not about arrogance or self-reliance but about a confidence deeply rooted in God's promises and power. Boldness in the divine handshake means stepping into the unknown, confident that God's hand is stretched out in partnership with us. It means understanding that we are not alone and that God's strength is made perfect in our weakness (2 Corinthians 12:9).

In Moody's time, his ministry required this type of fearless confidence. When he ventured to England to preach, he was initially met with skepticism and opposition. Many questioned his qualifications, his lack of formal theological education, and his unconventional methods. Yet, Moody's confidence was not in his own ability but in the God who had called him. He understood that a divine partnership with God meant embracing risks and trusting that God would provide the necessary power and wisdom.

Faith That Stretches Beyond Comfort Zones

Hebrews 11, often referred to as the "Hall of Faith," provides a compelling narrative of men and women who embraced the divine handshake and made bold plans with God. Their lives were characterized by faith that ventured beyond their comfort zones. Hebrews 11:6 states:

"And without faith, it is impossible to please God because anyone who comes to him must believe that he exists and that he rewards those who earnestly seek him."

Moody lived by this principle. His vision for ministry was always beyond what seemed reasonable or achievable. When he began his Sunday school for street kids in Chicago, he faced constant criticism and lacked financial resources. However, his faith was not in what he could see but in the unseen God who rewards those who seek Him diligently. Moody knew that the essence of the divine handshake was the invitation to trust God for the impossible.

This same invitation is extended to us today. In our modern context, the temptation is to play it safe—to make plans that are manageable and comfortable. Yet, God is calling us to dream bigger and stretch our faith further. The divine handshake compels us to partner with God in ways that demand His supernatural intervention. We are reminded in Ephesians 3:20:

"Now to him who is able to do immeasurably more than all we ask or imagine, according to his power that is at work within us."

This scripture reveals that God's ability to work through us is only limited by the size of our faith and our willingness to act. The divine handshake is an invitation to expand our imagination and make room for God to move in extraordinary ways.

Practical Steps to Making Big Plans with God

While dreaming big is essential, it must be coupled with practical steps of obedience and faith. The following steps can help guide us in making big plans with God:

1. **Align with God's Heart**: Before making any plans, seek God's heart and ask Him to reveal His will. Jeremiah 29:13 encourages us, "You will seek me and find me when you seek me with all your heart." Begin with a posture of surrender, asking God to align your desires with His purposes.

2. **Cultivate Boldness Through Prayer and the Word**: The boldness needed to make big plans with God is cultivated through a life saturated in prayer and Scripture. Hebrews 4:16 says, "Let us then approach God's throne of grace with confidence, so that we may receive mercy and find grace to help us in our time of need." Prayer positions us to hear from God and receive the courage to act.
3. **Step Out in Faith**: Big plans require significant steps of faith. Faith is not passive; it is active. James 2:26 reminds us, "As the body without the spirit is dead, so faith without deeds is dead." Once God reveals His plans, step out in obedience, even when the path is unclear.
4. **Embrace God's Timing**: Bold plans must also be tempered with patience. Ecclesiastes 3:11 states, "He has made everything beautiful in its time." Trusting God's timing is crucial in the divine handshake. Waiting does not mean inaction; it means preparation and trust.
5. **Partner with Others**: God often uses community to accomplish His plans. Ecclesiastes 4:9 reminds us, "Two are better than one because they have a good return for their labor." Surround yourself with like-minded believers who encourage and support God-sized dreams.
6. **Stay Humble and Teachable**: As God begins to unfold His plans, maintain a posture of humility and teachability. Proverbs 11:2 warns, "When pride comes, then comes disgrace, but with humility comes wisdom." The divine handshake is an ongoing process of learning and growing.

Understanding the Role of the Holy Spirit

The Holy Spirit is the enabler of the divine handshake. Just as the Spirit descended upon Jesus at His baptism, empowering Him for ministry under an open heaven, the Spirit empowers us to live boldly for God. Acts 1:8 declares:

"But you will receive power when the Holy Spirit comes on you; and you will be my witnesses in Jerusalem, and in all Judea and Samaria, and to the ends of the earth."

Living under an open heaven means walking in the power and authority of the Holy Spirit. This power is not just for personal edification but for fulfilling God's mission on earth. It is the Spirit who gives us the courage to make bold plans and the wisdom to execute them effectively. When we embrace the Spirit's leading, we enter a dynamic partnership with God where the impossible becomes possible.

The Cost of Playing It Safe

There is a cost to playing it safe in our walk with God. When we limit our plans to what we can achieve on our own, we miss out on experiencing the fullness of God's power and purpose. A.W. Tozer famously said, "God is looking for those with whom He can do the impossible." How tragic that many believers never step into this reality because they are afraid to take risks.

Consider the parable of the talents in Matthew 25:14-30. The servant who buried his talent played it safe, but his fear led to judgment. Conversely, those who invested their talents received commendation and reward. The divine handshake challenges us to invest all that we have in God's Kingdom, trusting that He will multiply our efforts.

The Joy of Co-Laboring with God

There is immense joy in co-laboring with God. When we see His hand at work in our lives and in the lives of others, our faith is strengthened, and our vision expanded. Philippians 2:13 reminds us:

"For it is God who works in you to will and to act in order to fulfill his good purpose."

God takes pleasure in working through His children to accomplish His purposes on earth. When we partner with Him in faith, we experience the joy of seeing lives transformed, communities impacted, and His Kingdom advanced. This joy far outweighs the temporary comforts of playing it safe.

Expanding Our Vision Through the Divine Handshake

D.L. Moody's life was marked by an unyielding faith that embraced the divine handshake. His legacy challenges us to dream big, trust boldly, and act fearlessly. The divine handshake invites each of us into a partnership with God that defies human logic and exceeds natural limitations.

As we make plans with God, let us remember that boldness, faith, and reliance on the Holy Spirit are essential components of this divine partnership. God is ready to do great things through those who are willing to take Him at His word and step out into the unknown. The question is, are you prepared to extend your hand in faith and see what God will do?

Let us echo the words of Isaiah 6:8:

** "Then I heard the voice of the Lord saying, 'Whom shall I send?'"

The Divine Handshake as an Invitation to Transformation

The divine handshake is more than just a partnership—it's an invitation to transformation. It is not merely about what we can do with God but about who we become as we co-labor with Him. This transformative journey begins with a shift in mindset, a renewal of the heart, and an alignment of our desires with God's purposes. Romans 12:2 reminds us:

"Do not conform to the pattern of this world, but be transformed by the renewing of your mind. Then you will be able to test and approve what God's will is—his good, pleasing, and perfect will."

When we partner with God, we allow Him to mold us into His image, transforming our fears into faith, our doubts into declarations of His power, and our small thinking into God-sized visions. This transformation is not a one-time event but an ongoing process of becoming more like Christ. As we continue to engage in the divine handshake, we experience more profound levels of growth, maturity, and effectiveness in our walk with God.

Cultivating a Culture of Bold Faith in Our Communities

The divine handshake is not just an individual calling; it is a collective invitation for the body of Christ to rise together in bold faith. As we step out in faith individually, we inspire and encourage others to do the same. The early church understood this principle well. Acts 4:31 records the power of their unified boldness:

"After they prayed, the place where they were meeting was shaken. And they were all filled with the Holy Spirit and spoke the word of God boldly."

This passage demonstrates the contagious nature of bold faith. When one person steps out, it encourages others to do the same. D.L. Moody's ministry was not just about his personal boldness but about igniting a generation to believe in God for more. His impact continues today because he invested in others and created a culture where bold faith was the norm.

As we pursue the divine handshake, we must also seek to cultivate this culture in our own churches and communities. We must encourage one another to take risks for the Kingdom, support each other in our

God-given assignments, and celebrate the steps of faith that lead to extraordinary outcomes. Hebrews 10:24-25 instructs us:

"And let us consider how we may spur one another on toward love and good deeds, not giving up meeting together, as some are in the habit of doing, but encouraging one another—and all the more as you see the Day approaching."

This verse underscores the importance of community in our walk of faith. The divine handshake is best experienced in the context of a supportive, faith-filled community where believers are committed to spurring one another on toward more significant things in God.

The Cost of the Divine Handshake: Counting the Cost of Discipleship

While the divine handshake offers us incredible opportunities to co-labor with God, it also comes with a cost. Jesus made it clear that following Him would require sacrifice, surrender, and a willingness to endure hardship for the sake of the Gospel. Luke 9:23-24 provides this challenge:

"Then he said to them all: 'Whoever wants to be my disciple must deny themselves and take up their cross daily and follow me. For whoever wants to save their life will lose it, but whoever loses their life for me will save it.'"

D.L. Moody understood that partnering with God was not a path of comfort but one of conviction. He faced numerous trials, including personal loss, financial challenges, and intense opposition. Yet, he never wavered in his commitment to God's calling. He counted the cost and found that what he gained in Christ far outweighed any earthly sacrifice. This is the essence of the divine handshake: a willingness to lay down our lives so that God's purposes can be fulfilled through us.

Living with Expectancy: Anticipating the Miraculous

To live in a divine handshake with God is to live with a sense of expectancy. It means waking up every day with the anticipation that God is going to move in powerful ways. This expectancy is not wishful thinking; it is a deep-seated faith that God is who He says He is and that He will do what He has promised. Ephesians 3:20 is a foundational verse for this kind of living:

"Now to him who is able to do immeasurably more than all we ask or imagine, according to his power that is at work within us."

When we align our lives with this truth, we open ourselves up to the miraculous. We begin to see opportunities where others see obstacles. We start to pray for the impossible because we know that with God, all things are possible. This is the essence of the divine handshake—living with the expectancy that God will show up and do what only He can do.

Bold Plans Require Bold Prayers

One of the hallmarks of D.L. Moody's ministry was his commitment to bold, faith-filled prayer. He understood that big plans require big prayers. Prayer is the engine that drives the divine handshake. It is in the place of prayer that we receive God's vision, hear His voice, and gain the courage to act. James 5:16 reminds us:

"The prayer of a righteous person is powerful and effective."

Bold prayers are not timid or half-hearted; they are prayers that stretch our faith and align us with God's purposes. They are prayers that move mountains and bring heaven to earth. As we enter into the divine handshake with God, we must commit ourselves to a lifestyle of bold, persistent prayer. It is in the place of worship that our plans are birthed, shaped, and empowered by God's Spirit.

The Role of Obedience in Co-Laboring with God

Another essential component of the divine handshake is obedience. Bold plans and bold prayers must be coupled with bold obedience. It is not enough to dream big; we must be willing to act on what God has revealed. Jesus said in John 14:15:

"If you love me, keep my commands."

Obedience is the evidence of our love for God and our commitment to His plans. It is the practical outworking of our faith. When God called Moses to lead the Israelites out of Egypt, it required bold obedience. When He called Joshua to march around Jericho, it required bold obedience. When He called Peter to step out of the boat, it required bold obedience. The divine handshake is always accompanied by a call to action—a call to trust God enough to do what He says, even when it doesn't make sense.

God's Glory Revealed Through Our Boldness

One of the most profound truths of the divine handshake is that our boldness ultimately reveals God's glory. When we step out in faith, make big plans, and obey God's leading, we position ourselves for God to showcase His power and goodness. 2 Corinthians 4:7 reminds us:

"But we have this treasure in jars of clay to show that this all-surpassing power is from God and not from us."

God delights in using ordinary people to accomplish extraordinary things. He chooses the weak to shame the strong, the foolish to confound the wise, and the humble to exalt His name. When we embrace the divine handshake, we become vessels through which His glory is displayed. Our boldness becomes a testimony to His greatness, and our faith becomes a beacon that draws others to Him.

Stepping Into the Divine Adventure

The life and ministry of D.L. Moody serve as a potent reminder that God is still looking for men and women who will take Him at His word and make big plans with Him. The divine handshake is an invitation to step into a divine adventure—a journey marked by bold faith, courageous obedience, and the miraculous power of God.

As we conclude this chapter, let us be reminded that the divine handshake is not just a concept; it is a lifestyle. It is a call to live beyond ourselves, to dream beyond our limitations, and to act beyond our fears. It is an invitation to co-labor with the Creator of the universe in ways that impact eternity.

God is extending His hand to you today. Will you take it? Will you make plans so big that only God can fulfill them? Will you trust Him enough to step out of the boat, face the giants, and march around the walls? The divine handshake awaits, and with it comes the promise of seeing God do "immeasurably more than all we ask or imagine."

Let us, like D.L. Moody, be bold enough to say, "If God is our partner, let's make our plans big!" And as we do, may we experience the fullness of His power, the depth of His love, and the glory of His presence in ways we never thought possible.

Additional Scriptures to Reflect On:
- **Joshua 1:9**—"Have I not commanded you? Be strong and courageous. Do not be afraid; do not be discouraged, for the Lord your God will be with you wherever you go."
- **Matthew 17:20**—"He replied, 'Because you have so little faith. Truly, I tell you, if you have faith as small as a mustard seed, you can say to this mountain, 'Move from here to there,' and it will move. Nothing will be impossible for you.'"
- **Isaiah 41:10**—"So do not fear, for I am with you; do not be dismayed, for I am your God. I will strengthen you and help you; I will uphold you with my righteous right hand."

- **2 Timothy 1:7**—"For the Spirit God gave us does not make us timid, but gives us power, love, and self-discipline."

These scriptures reinforce the truth that God is calling us to a life of boldness and courage. His Spirit empowers us to live fearlessly, to dream audaciously, and to take risks for His Kingdom. The divine handshake is an invitation to live in a way that continually reaches for the extraordinary, trusting in God's ability to do the impossible through us.

Dream Big, Act Boldly

As you consider your life, your calling, and the opportunities before you, remember that God is not looking for people who will play it safe. He is searching for those who will embrace the divine handshake, step into the unknown, and make plans that require His power to accomplish. Your life, like D.L. Moody's, can become a testimony of what God can do through a surrendered vessel.

So, what will your response be? Will you make your plans big, knowing that God is your partner? Will you allow your faith to stretch beyond your comfort zone and trust God to meet you in the place of the impossible? The divine handshake is extended to you today—grab hold of it and never let go. Let your life be marked by bold faith, audacious plans, and a deep reliance on the God who is able to do exceedingly, abundantly above all that we could ask or imagine.

"Here I am, Lord. Send me. Use me. Change me. Make your plans my plans, and let your will be done in my life as it is in heaven."

CHAPTER 11

The Dynamic Partnership of Prayer and Divine Purpose

The lives and ministries of J. Oswald Sanders and John Wesley exemplify a profound understanding of the divine partnership between God and humanity. Both men, through their teachings and writings, emphasized the irreplaceable role of human cooperation with God's will, primarily through prayer. Their insights beautifully align with the concept of the Divine Handshake—the mutual exchange between heaven and earth, where God extends His hand to humanity, inviting us to partner with Him in fulfilling His purposes.

J. Oswald Sanders: A Life Committed to the Power of Prayer

J. Oswald Sanders (1902–1992) was a spiritual leader, author, and missionary who profoundly impacted Christian thought on prayer, leadership, and discipleship. Born in New Zealand, Sanders was a prominent figure in the Christian & Missionary Alliance, serving as the general director of the Overseas Missionary Fellowship, formerly the China Inland Mission. Throughout his life, he exhibited a passion for encouraging believers to live lives of intimacy with God, mainly through prayer.

In his writings, especially in his influential book "Prayer Power Unlimited," Sanders explores the depths of prayer as a cooperative act between man and God. His quote, "God has forever tied Himself to human cooperation for the execution of divine purposes," underscores a critical element of his theology. For Sanders, prayer is not merely a religious duty or a pious habit but a dynamic, collaborative process.

God has sovereignly chosen to involve humanity in His divine plans. Through prayer, we enter into a sacred partnership with God—a Divine Handshake—that brings His will into reality on earth.

Sanders' ministry revolved around the concept that God does not force His will upon the earth without the cooperative efforts of His people. He believed that prayer is the conduit through which the power and plans of God flow into our world. Just as Jesus taught His disciples to pray, "Your kingdom come, You will be done, on earth as it is in heaven" (Matthew 6:10), Sanders emphasized that God's kingdom purposes are actualized when His people pray and cooperate with His Spirit.

His life was marked by a deep commitment to prayer and a reliance on God's leading. Sanders knew that effective leadership in God's kingdom could not rely on human wisdom or strength alone. Instead, it required a deep dependence on God through prayer—a theme he wrote about extensively and lived out in his daily life. His books, lectures, and personal examples have inspired countless believers to embrace their role in the divine partnership of prayer, recognizing that God's hand moves in response to the prayers of His people.

John Wesley: The Founder of Methodism and the Power of Intercessory Prayer

John Wesley (1703–1791), the renowned evangelist, theologian, and founder of the Methodist movement, is another towering figure in church history who understood the necessity of human cooperation for divine purposes. Wesley's life and ministry were characterized by an unyielding emphasis on prayer, holiness, and evangelism. His quote, "God does nothing but in answer to prayer," captures the essence of his theological perspective on the relationship between God and humanity.

For Wesley, prayer was the driving force behind all of God's activity on earth. He believed that while God is sovereign and can act independently, He has ordained that much of His work is contingent upon human prayer. This belief shaped his entire ministry strategy, making prayer the foundation of the Methodist revival in England. Wesley's theological framework viewed prayer as not merely a means of communicating with God but as an essential partnership between the Creator and His creation. He believed that without human intercession, God's will would not be fully realized on earth.

Wesley's life was a testament to the power of prayerful partnership with God. He traveled extensively, preaching the gospel and calling for repentance and holiness. His ministry saw thousands converted, churches planted, and societies transformed. Yet, behind all these visible successes was a man who spent hours in prayer, often rising early in the morning and spending time on his knees before his day began. Wesley understood that the true power behind any move of God was birthed and sustained in prayer.

One of Wesley's enduring legacies is the emphasis on "the means of grace," mainly corporate and private prayer, as vital practices for all believers. He taught that through these means, Christians grow in grace and become partners with God in His redemptive work. For Wesley, prayer was more than a ritual; it was an act of co-laboring with God. It was through prayer that believers became participants in the divine life and co-architects with God in shaping history.

The Divine Handshake in the Lives of Sanders and Wesley

Both J. Oswald Sanders and John Wesley exemplify the Divine Handshake—a sacred partnership where God invites us to join Him in His work through the vehicle of prayer. Their lives demonstrate that God has chosen to move on earth in cooperation with His people, not apart from them. This understanding has profound implications for how we live, pray, and engage with God's purposes today.

Sanders' assertion that "God has forever tied Himself to human cooperation for the execution of divine purposes" aligns perfectly with Wesley's conviction that "God does nothing but in answer to prayer." Both men understood that God, in His sovereignty, has designed a system where our prayers and actions matter. They believed that our role is not passive but active; we are called to engage in a divine partnership where our prayers, faith, and actions align with God's will to bring about His kingdom's purposes on earth.

Boldness in Prayer: Co-Laboring with God

The Divine Handshake calls us to boldness in prayer. Just as Sanders and Wesley taught, prayer is not merely a petition for God to act; it is an invitation to participate with Him in His work. In the book of **Hebrews 4:16**, we are encouraged: "Let us then approach God's throne of grace with confidence, so that we may receive mercy and find grace to help us in our time of need." This passage speaks of boldness and confidence in prayer, knowing that we are co-laborers with God in fulfilling His purposes.

In the same vein, **1 John 5:14-15** states, "This is the confidence we have in approaching God: that if we ask anything according to His will, He hears us. And if we know that He hears us—whatever we ask—we know that we have what we asked of Him." The divine partnership that Sanders and Wesley spoke of is grounded in this confidence—that God hears and responds to the prayers of His people.

The Role of Faith in the Divine Handshake

Faith is the currency of the Kingdom. Both Sanders and Wesley lived lives marked by deep, abiding faith in God's promises. They believed that through faith-filled prayer, God's purposes were made manifest on earth. The divine handshake requires that we believe in God's character, promises, and power.

The writer of **Hebrews 11:6** reminds us, "And without faith, it is impossible to please God because anyone who comes to him must believe that he exists and that he rewards those who earnestly seek him." Faith is essential to the divine handshake. It is the substance that activates heaven's response to our prayers.

Furthermore, **James 5:16** declares, "The prayer of a righteous person is powerful and effective." Sanders and Wesley lived in the reality that their prayers, fueled by faith and righteousness, had the power to move mountains and shift spiritual atmospheres. This is the essence of the divine handshake—a powerful, effective partnership between heaven and earth.

Prayer as a Catalyst for Divine Action

In the lives of Sanders and Wesley, prayer was the catalyst for divine action. It was not a passive activity but a powerful weapon that brought about change. Wesley's revival meetings and Sanders' missionary endeavors were marked by intense, focused prayer that called down heaven's power and presence.

2 Chronicles 7:14 illustrates this principle well: "If my people, who are called by my name, will humble themselves and pray and seek my face and turn from their wicked ways, then I will hear from heaven, and I will forgive their sin and will heal their land." Prayer is the catalyst for divine intervention. It is the means by which God's hand moves in our world.

Both Sanders and Wesley knew that prayer changes things—not because of the eloquence of the words spoken but because of the One to whom we pray. They understood that God's power is released through prayer and that He has chosen to partner with us in this divine process.

The Divine Handshake and the Call to Intercession

Sanders and Wesley also knew that the divine handshake involves intercession—a form of prayer that stands in the gap for others. They believed that God had called His people to be intercessors, to pray for the lost, the hurting, and the broken. Through intercession, we partner with God in seeing His kingdom come and His will be done on earth.

Isaiah 59:16 says, "He saw that there was no one, he was appalled that there was no one to intervene; so his own arm achieved salvation for him, and his own righteousness sustained him." God is looking for intercessors, those who will stand in the gap and partner with Him in prayer for His purposes to be accomplished.

Sanders, in his writings, emphasized the power of intercessory prayer and its role in the divine partnership. Wesley, too, was known for his tireless intercession for revival, salvation, and societal transformation. They understood that intercession is a crucial aspect of the divine handshake, where heaven and earth meet to bring about God's will.

Embracing the Divine Partnership

The lives and teachings of J. Oswald Sanders and John Wesley offer us profound insights into the nature of our relationship with God. They remind us that God has chosen to involve us in His plans through prayer. The divine handshake is an invitation to enter into a partnership with God, where our prayers, faith, and actions align with His will to bring about divine purposes on earth.

Their lives teach us that we are not passive recipients of God's work but active participants. This partnership is built on the foundation of prayer—an intimate dialogue with God where we not only speak but also listen, discern, and align our hearts with His. Both Sanders and Wesley illustrate that the effectiveness of our prayers is not measured by our ability but by our willingness to cooperate with God's divine plan.

As believers, we are called to embrace this divine handshake fully. We must commit to a lifestyle of bold, faith-filled prayer, knowing that God has forever tied Himself to human cooperation for the execution of His divine purposes. Our prayers become the very vessels that carry His plans from heaven to earth, allowing us to see His kingdom come and His will be done.

A Call to Action

Now, more than ever, we must rise to the challenge set before us by these great men of faith. We must be willing to co-labor with God, making bold plans that reflect His greatness, trusting Him for the impossible, and embracing our role as partners in His redemptive mission on earth. This is the essence of the Divine Handshake—a relationship where heaven meets earth, where God extends His hand to us, and we, in faith and obedience, grasp it with all our might.

May we, like Sanders and Wesley, become vessels through which God's purposes flow. Let us answer the call to prayer, intercession, and faith-filled action, knowing that through this divine partnership, the impossible becomes possible, and heaven touches earth. This is our calling. This is the Divine Handshake.

CHAPTER 12

The Legacy of Co-Laboring with God

The unfolding story of God's work on earth is marked by an extraordinary truth: God chooses to accomplish His divine purposes through human cooperation. Throughout the ages, God has invited men and women to participate in His work, even though He could achieve it all by Himself. This is a profound mystery—a divine handshake—where the sovereign power of God meets human willingness, allowing the ordinary to touch the extraordinary. Some of history's most notable spiritual leaders have deeply understood this divine partnership. C.S. Lewis, Watchman Nee, A.W. Tozer, and Corrie ten Boom all grasped this concept in their unique ways, offering insights that still resonate today.

C.S. Lewis: The Humble Intellect

C.S. Lewis, a towering figure in Christian apologetics, profoundly understood the divine-human partnership. Known for his ability to blend intellectual rigor with imaginative storytelling, Lewis once said, "For He seems to do nothing of Himself which He can possibly delegate to His creatures. He commands us to do slowly and blunderingly what He could do perfectly in the twinkling of an eye" (*The World's Last Night*). This quote encapsulates Lewis's realization that God, who could perform His work perfectly and instantaneously, instead chooses to work through the slow and often flawed efforts of human beings.

Lewis's life was a journey from atheism to Christianity, marked by a reluctant but total surrender to God. His conversion was not merely an intellectual decision but a deep acknowledgment of God's call to co-labor with Him. The writings that flowed from this surrender—*Mere Christianity, The Chronicles of Narnia, The Problem of Pain*—are all works that reflect his partnership with God. Lewis was not content merely to write as an intellectual exercise; he saw his work as an act of divine cooperation. His ability to communicate profound truths in ways that stirred both the mind and the heart demonstrated how God could use a "slow and blundering" human being to perform work that resonates across generations. In this way, Lewis mirrors the life of Watchman Nee, who, despite different cultural and contextual challenges, also saw the value in surrendering to divine cooperation.

"For we are God's fellow workers; you are God's field, God's building." (1 Corinthians 3:9, ESV)

Watchman Nee: The Suffering Servant

Watchman Nee, an influential Christian leader and author from China, emphasized the necessity of living in cooperation with the indwelling Christ. "The normal Christian life must be one of living in cooperation with the indwelling Christ," he wrote. Unlike Lewis, who operated within the freedom of Western academia, Nee ministered under intense persecution. His message was shaped by a deep understanding of the cost of discipleship. For Nee, co-laboring with God was not about grand acts of visible service; it was about the daily, often hidden, cooperation with Christ within.

Nee's most influential work, *The Normal Christian Life*, speaks to this need for a life lived in partnership with God. His teachings often emphasized the believer's union with Christ—"Christ in you, the hope of glory" (Colossians 1:27). This was not just theology for Nee; it was reality. Imprisoned for the last 20 years of his life, he could no longer preach publicly, but he continued to write, pray, and remain in deep fellowship with God. His hidden labor was no less valuable than his public ministry. Like Lewis, Nee's life shows that God's work is not limited to platforms or pulpits. Both men, though different in context, illuminate how God chooses to involve humans in His work, knowing that this partnership is as much about forming the worker as it is about completing the task.

"To them, God has chosen to make known among the Gentiles the glorious riches of this mystery, which is Christ in you, the hope of glory." (Colossians 1:27, NIV)

A.W. Tozer: The Prophet of the Impossible

A.W. Tozer, a pastor and theologian known for his uncompromising call to spiritual depth, echoed similar themes of divine-human cooperation. "God is looking for people through whom He can do the impossible. What a pity that we plan only the things we can do by ourselves," Tozer said. This statement reflects a profound challenge to believers: to break free from a self-reliant mindset and embrace the adventure of faith that requires dependence on God.

Tozer's ministry, although different in style from Lewis and Nee's, shared the same core understanding of co-laboring with God. He had no formal theological education, yet he authored many books that have profoundly impacted the Christian world, such as *The Pursuit of God* and *The Knowledge of the Holy*. Tozer believed that the church often settles for mediocrity when God is inviting His people to trust Him for the impossible. His challenge mirrors the life of Corrie ten Boom, who also learned the profound truth of relying on God's strength rather than her own. Where Tozer saw the church's potential for greatness in divine partnership, Corrie lived out that truth in her own remarkable journey.

"Now to him who is able to do immeasurably more than all we ask or imagine, according to his power that is at work within us." (Ephesians 3:20, NIV)

Corrie ten Boom: The Spirit-Filled Survivor

Corrie ten Boom, a woman who survived the unimaginable horrors of a Nazi concentration camp, understood the futility of working on one's own strength. She poignantly stated, "Trying to do the Lord's work in your own strength is the most confusing, exhausting, and tedious of all work. But when you are filled with the Holy Spirit, then the ministry of Jesus just flows out of you." Corrie's life became a powerful example of how God uses those who depend entirely on Him.

During World War II, Corrie and her family hid Jews in their home, risking their lives in a profound act of co-laboring with God. When she was eventually arrested and sent to a concentration camp, Corrie discovered that even in the darkest place, God's work could continue. She learned that human strength is insufficient against the evil and suffering of the world, but God's strength, when entirely relied upon, becomes a river of life. After the war, she traveled the world, speaking of forgiveness, healing, and the power of the Holy Spirit. Her ministry was not something she orchestrated on her own; it was a natural outflow of God's Spirit within her. Her life resonates with the message of Watchman Nee, whose emphasis on the indwelling Christ aligns perfectly with Corrie's own experiences of divine partnership in suffering and beyond.

"But he said to me, 'My grace is sufficient for you, for my power is made perfect in weakness.' Therefore, I will boast all the more gladly of my weaknesses so that the power of Christ may rest upon me." (2 Corinthians 12:9, ESV)

The Divine Handshake

Reflecting on the lives of Lewis, Nee, Tozer, and Ten Boom, we see a beautiful tapestry of what it means to co-labor with God. Each one, from their unique vantage point, understood that God's invitation to partner with Him is not about human achievement but divine transformation. Lewis's intellectual surrender, Nee's hidden perseverance,

Tozer's prophetic call to faith, and Corrie's reliance on the Spirit all point to one central truth: God's work is accomplished when we place our hands in His.

Their lives teach us that God's desire is not for us to do great things *for* Him but to do great things *with* Him. When we partner with God, we are not merely tools in His hands; we are His beloved children invited into His redemptive story. The synergy of divine sovereignty and human agency is a mystery—a handshake between heaven and earth. We are not called to be passive observers but active participants in the unfolding of God's Kingdom.

Matthew 6:10, ESV— *"Your kingdom come, your will be done, on earth as it is in heaven."*

In this divine partnership, we find our true identity and purpose. We learn that our weaknesses are not barriers but bridges for God's power to flow. We discover that our efforts, though imperfect, are made perfect in His hands. Let us not shy away from this invitation. Let us, like these great men and women of faith, embrace the call to co-labor with God. May we step out in faith, knowing that the God who calls us is the God who equips us. May our lives, like theirs, be marked by a deep, abiding partnership with the Creator so that His glory is revealed through us.

"Then I heard the voice of the Lord saying, 'Whom shall I send? And who will go for us?' And I said, 'Here am I. Send me!'" (Isaiah 6:8, NIV)

In the end, it is not about what we accomplish but who we become as we walk hand-in-hand with the Almighty. It is in this sacred partnership that the ordinary becomes extraordinary, and the mundane becomes miraculous. Heaven touches earth, and both are forever changed.

Appendix

Bible Translations and Scripture References
1. **New International Version (NIV)**
   - **2 Corinthians 6:1**: "As God's co-workers, we urge you not to receive God's grace in vain."
   - **1 Corinthians 3:9**: "For we are co-workers in God's service; you are God's field, God's building."
   - **Hebrews 4:16**: "Let us then approach God's throne of grace with confidence, so that we may receive mercy and find grace to help us in our time of need."
   - **Matthew 6:10**: "Your kingdom come, your will be done, on earth as it is in heaven."
   - **Philippians 2:10-11**: "That at the name of Jesus every knee should bow, in heaven and on earth and under the earth, and every tongue acknowledge that Jesus Christ is Lord, to the glory of God the Father."

2. **English Standard Version (ESV)**
   - **John 15:14-15**: "You are my friends if you do what I command you. I no longer call you servants, for the servant does not know what his master is doing, but I have called you friends."
   - **Ephesians 2:10**: "For we are His workmanship, created in Christ Jesus for good works, which God prepared beforehand that we should walk in them."
   - **Romans 12:2**: "Do not conform to the pattern of this world, but be transformed by the renewing of your mind."
   - **Revelation 21:6**: "He said to me: 'It is done. I am the Alpha and the Omega, the Beginning and the End. To the

thirsty I will give water without cost from the spring of the water of life.'"

3. **New King James Version (NKJV)**
   - **James 4:8**: "Draw near to God, and He will draw near to you."
   - **Matthew 28:18-20**: "Then Jesus came to them and said, 'All authority in heaven and on earth has been given to me. Therefore, go and make disciples of all nations… And surely I am with you always, to the very end of the age.'"
   - **Psalm 37:4**: "Delight yourself also in the Lord, and He shall give you the desires of your heart."
   - **Proverbs 13:12**: "Hope deferred makes the heart sick, but a desire fulfilled is a tree of life."

4. **Amplified Bible (AMP)**
   - **Hebrews 10:35-36**: "Do not, therefore, fling away your [fearless] confidence, for it has a glorious and great reward. For you have need of patient endurance [to bear up under difficult circumstances without compromising], so that when you have carried out the will of God, you may receive and enjoy to the full what is promised."

5. **New Living Translation (NLT)**
   - **Revelation 3:20**: "Here I am! I stand at the door and knock. If anyone hears my voice and opens the door, I will come in and eat with that person, and they with me."

6. **King James Version (KJV)**
   - **Genesis 1:1**: "In the beginning, God created the heavens and the earth."
   - **John 15:5**: "I am the vine; you are the branches. If you remain in Me and I in you, you will bear much fruit; apart from Me you can do nothing."

- **Romans 11:36**: "For from Him and through Him and to Him are all things. To Him be the glory forever."

Authors and Quotes

1. **J. Oswald Sanders**
   - Quote: "God has forever tied Himself to human cooperation for the execution of divine purposes."
   - Source: *Prayer Power Unlimited* by J. Oswald Sanders, Moody Publishers.

2. **John Wesley**
   - Quote: "God does nothing but in answer to prayer."
   - Source: John Wesley's writings on prayer and Christian life, particularly in his sermons and theological works.

3. **D.L. Moody**
   - Quote: "If God is your partner, make your plans big."
   - Source: Writings and teachings of Dwight L. Moody, particularly in his collected sermons and revival messages.

4. **A.W. Tozer**
   - Quote: "God is looking for those with whom He can do the impossible—what a pity that we plan only the things that we can do by ourselves."
   - Source: *The Pursuit of God* by A.W. Tozer, Christian Publications.

5. **Jerry Bridges**
   - Quote: "Faith in Christ and a reliance on ourselves, even to the smallest degree, are mutually exclusive."
   - Source: *The Pursuit of Holiness* by Jerry Bridges, NavPress.

Greek Words

1. **Doulos (Greek:** δοῦλος**)**
    - Meaning: Servant or slave; used in the New Testament to describe a bond-servant or one who is bound to serve.

2. **Panim (Hebrew:** פנים**)**
    - Meaning: Face or presence; reflects the multidimensional nature of God's presence.

3. **Schizo (Greek:** σχίζω**)**
    - Meaning: To tear, divide, or split; used in Mark 1:10 and Matthew 27:51 to describe the tearing of the heavens or the temple veil.

About the Author

Manny Rivera, alongside his wife **Victoria**, has been a transformative leader in ministry for over three decades. Together, they have planted four thriving churches and traveled across the globe, speaking at conferences and training leaders in both ministry and marketplace settings. Manny currently serves as the Lead Pastor of Discover Life Church in Lawrenceville, Georgia, where his impact continues to ripple through the lives of his congregation and beyond.

Manny's ministry journey began in an unexpected place—a promising career in baseball. However, a life-altering encounter with Jesus radically changed his trajectory, compelling him to step away from sports and into full-time ministry. Since then, Manny has been driven by a singular passion: to ignite spiritual revival and raise up the next generation of leaders who will carry the fire of the Gospel.

For over 25 years, Manny has devoted himself to training and discipling both ministry and business leaders through his **Timothy Team**, a unique discipleship program designed for those seeking to fulfill God's call on their lives. His leadership is fueled by a relentless pursuit of revival, discipleship, and kingdom advancement. Known for his raw, unfiltered preaching style, Manny's messages are infused with the power of the Holy Spirit, consistently challenging people to live with conviction, purpose, and a deep connection to Christ.

Manny and Victoria are proud parents to four amazing adult children—**Calysta**, **Zayne**, **Zion** and his wife, **Erika**, and **Zealynd**—who continue to inspire them in their walk with God. Outside of ministry, Manny finds peace and rejuvenation in nature, often hiking and discovering new trails. His love for travel allows him to engage with diverse cultures and bring the message of Christ to the nations, whether he's speaking at international conferences or building relationships across the world.

Milton Keynes UK
Ingram Content Group UK Ltd.
UKHW031618231124
451036UK00004B/53